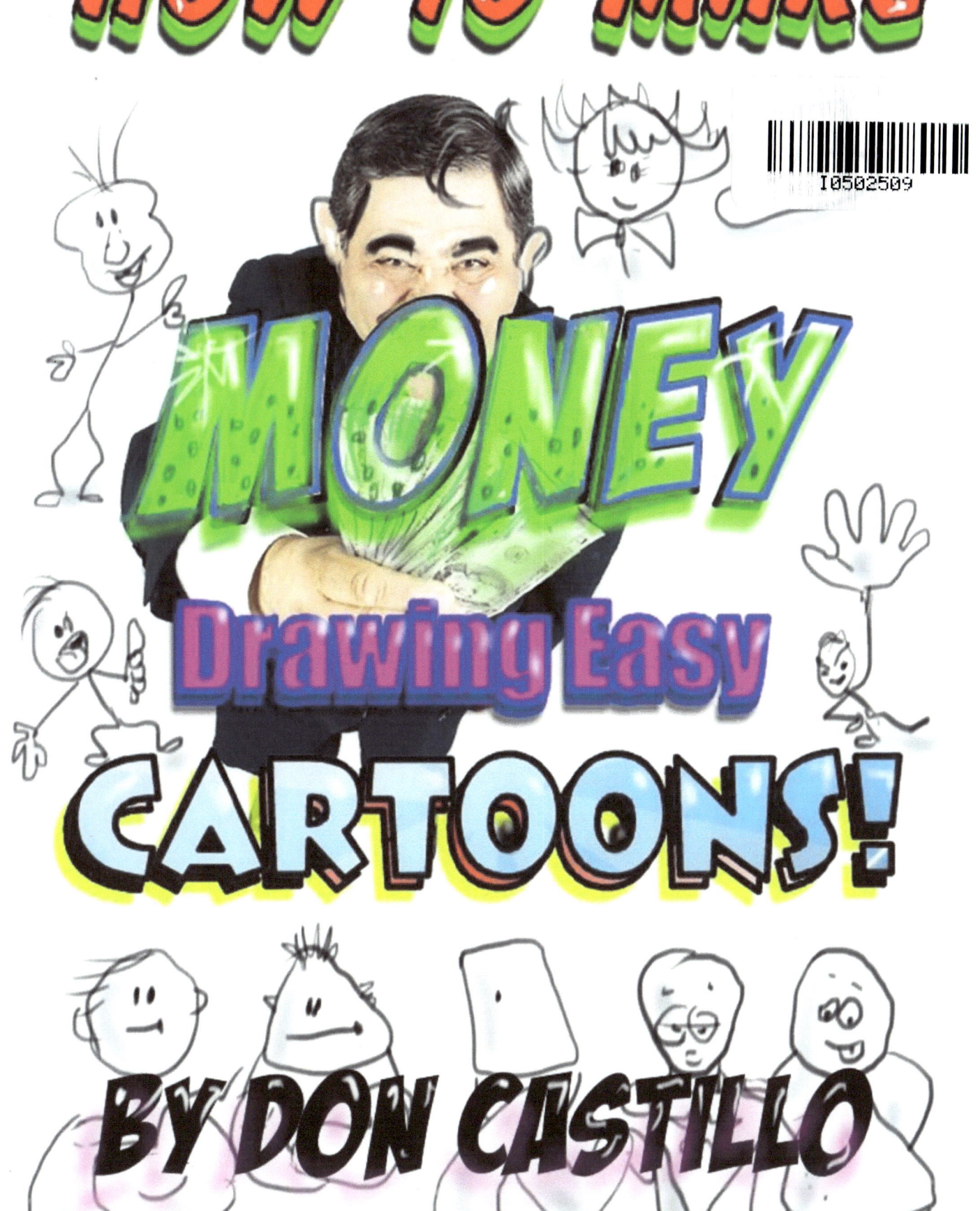

HOW TO MAKE
MONEY
Drawing Easy
CARTOONS!
BY DON CASTILLO

HOW TO MAKE MONEY DRAWING EASY CARTOONS!

CONTENTS...

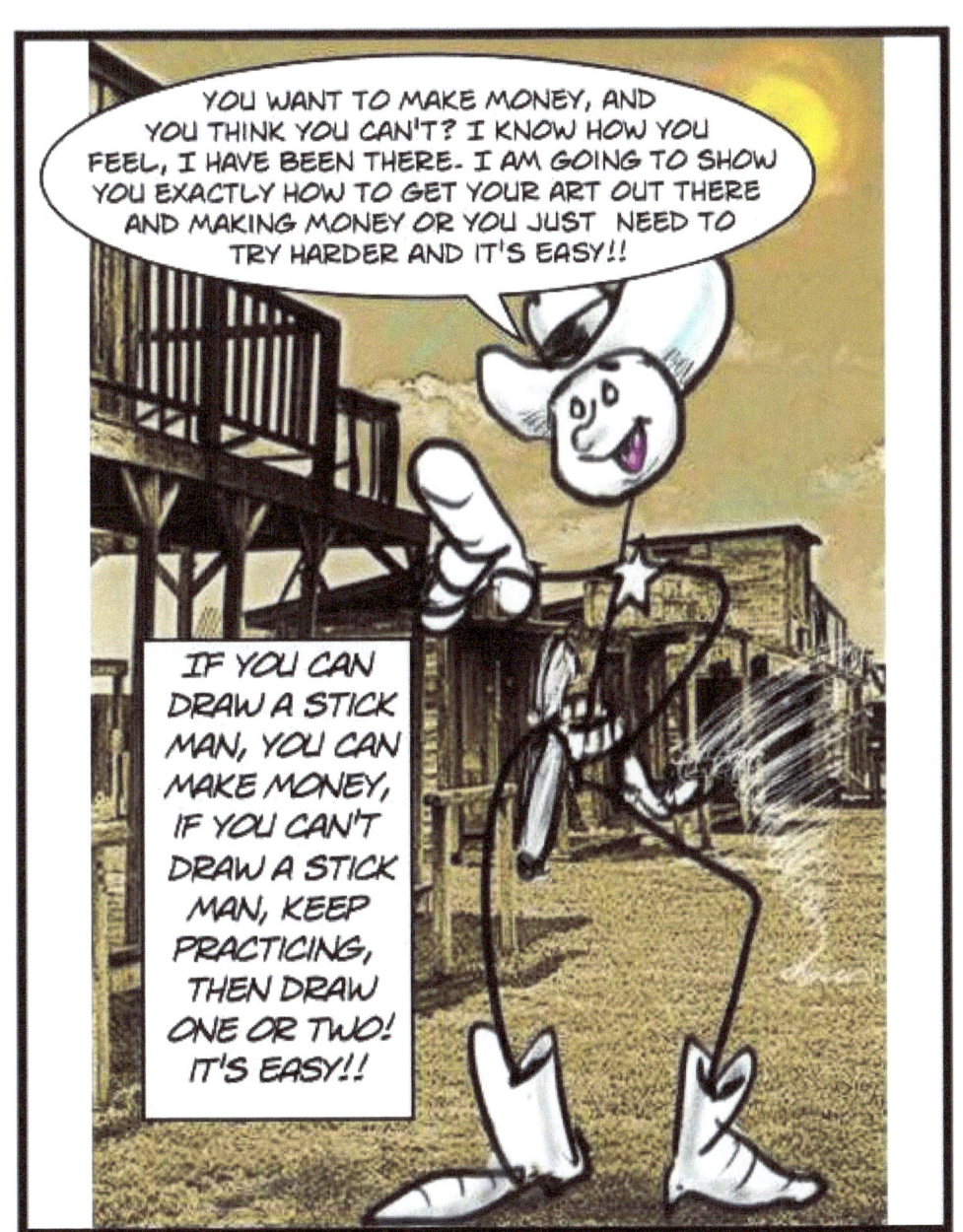

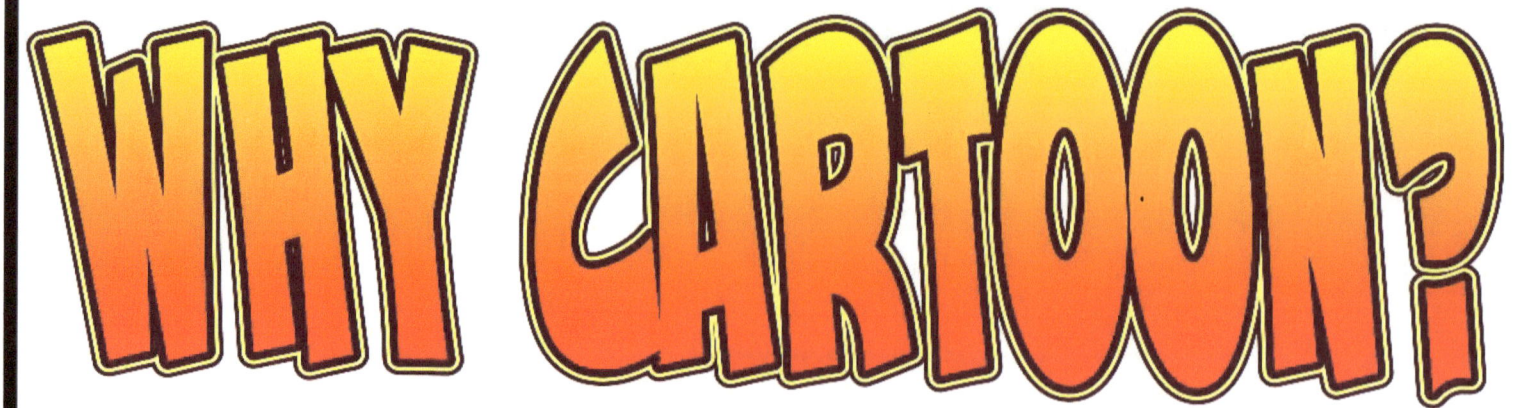

WHY CARTOON?

SOME OF US LIKE TO DRAW FOR FUN, WELL LET'S FACE IT, IF IT'S NOT FUN, WHY DO IT?

NOW I'M TELLING YOU, YOU CAN MAKE MONEY DOING IT, AND IN SOME CASES YOU DON'T EVEN HAVE TO DRAW!

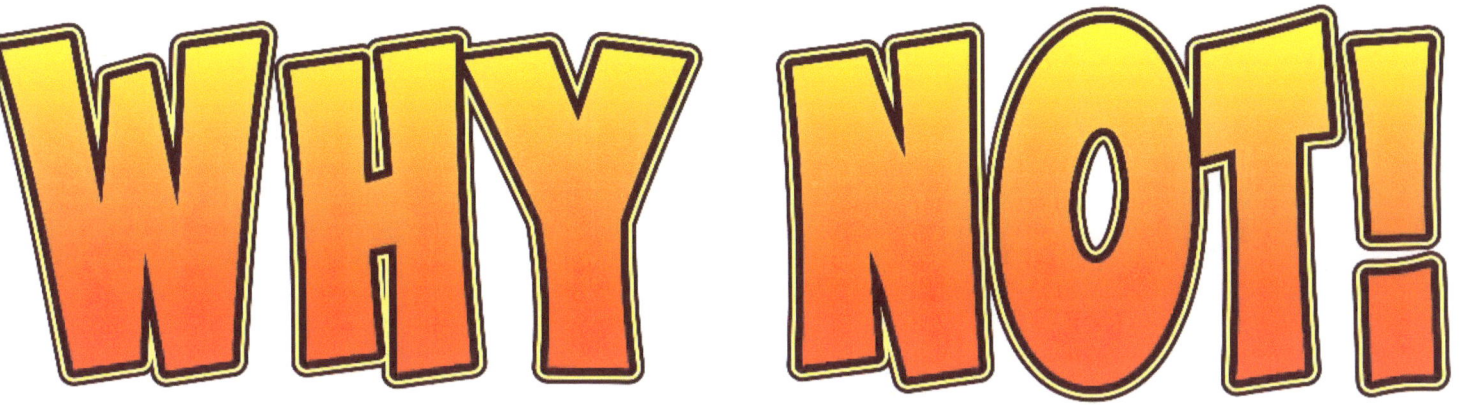

WHY NOT!

IF YOU NEVER DO ANYTHING, YOU WON'T EVER BE ANYTHING, OR MAKE ANY MONEY.

ALL I'M SAYING IS, WHY NOT WORK SMARTER NOT HARDER!
E-BOOKS ARE A GREAT WAY TO MAKE EASY MONEY!

MATERIALS

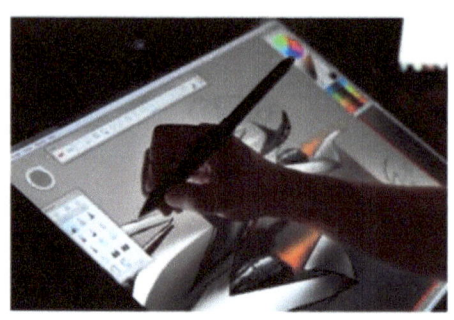

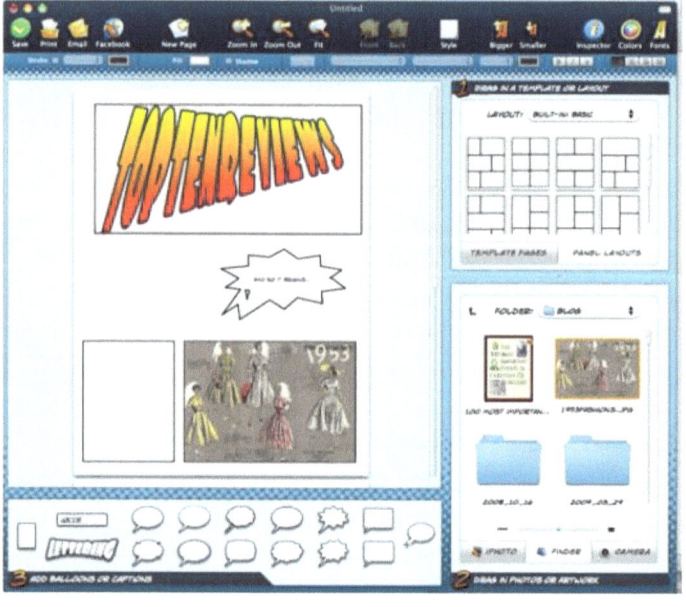

A DIGITAL TABLET IS NICE, BUT NOT NESSISARY, A SCANNER WILL DO AND ANY SIMPLE PAINT PROGRAM TO COLOR.

COMIC LIFE TO ADD CARTOON BALLOONS AND JAZZY TITLES.

INTERNET IS GREAT BUT YOU CAN MAIL SAMPLES OR TAKE THEM AROUND ON YOUR LAP TOP.

THINK OUTSIDE THE BOX!

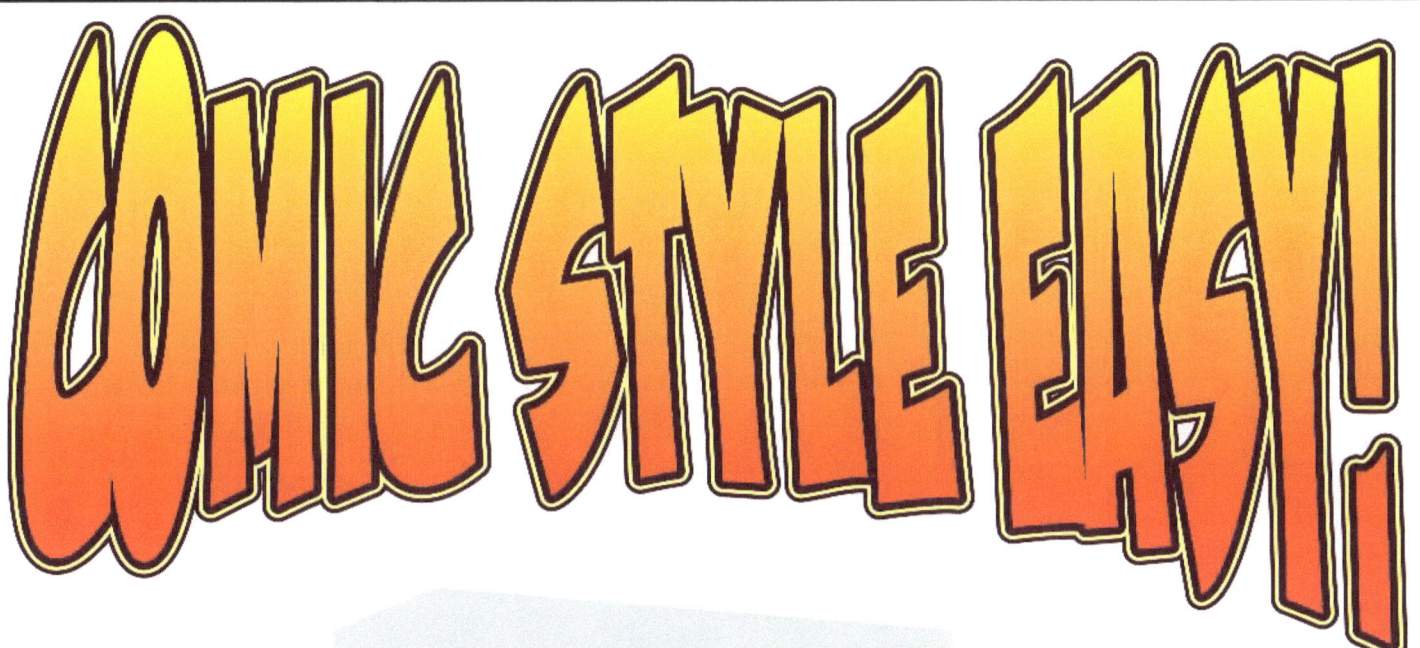

COMIC STYLE EASY!

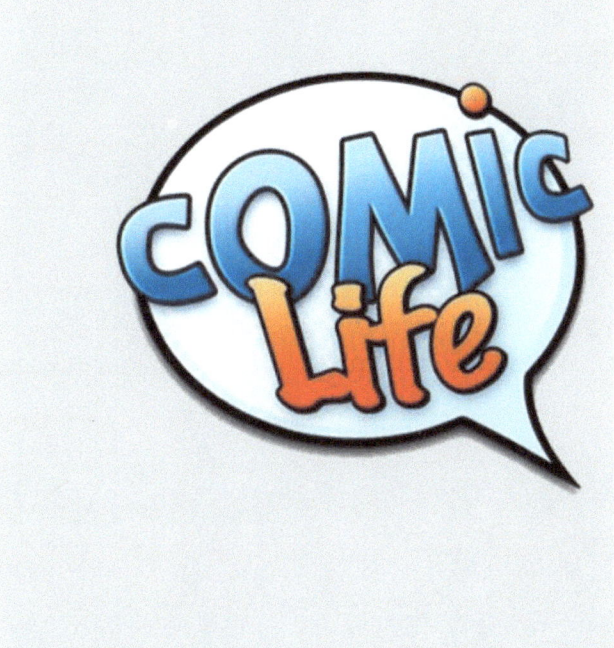

COMIC LIFE IS GREAT TO SET UP
YOUR COMIC OR E-BOOK.
I USE PHOTOS, CLIP ART, OR DRAW
WITH STICK FIGURES IF I NEED TO.

COMIC LIFE

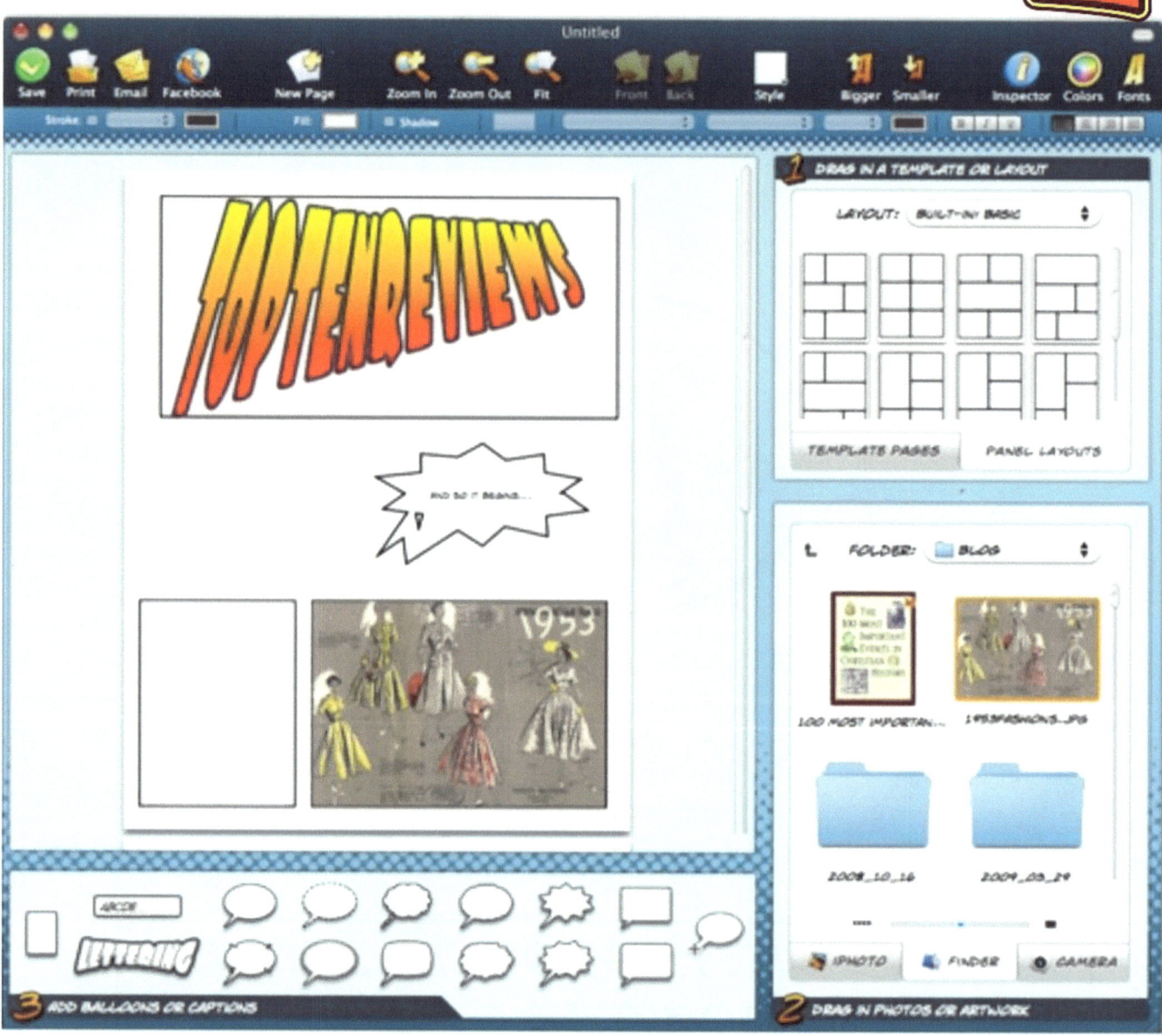

THIS IS A LAYOUT SCREEN SHOT FOR
COMIC LIFE.
MAKING MONEY WITH E-BOOKS IS
SO EASY, ANYONE CAN DO IT!

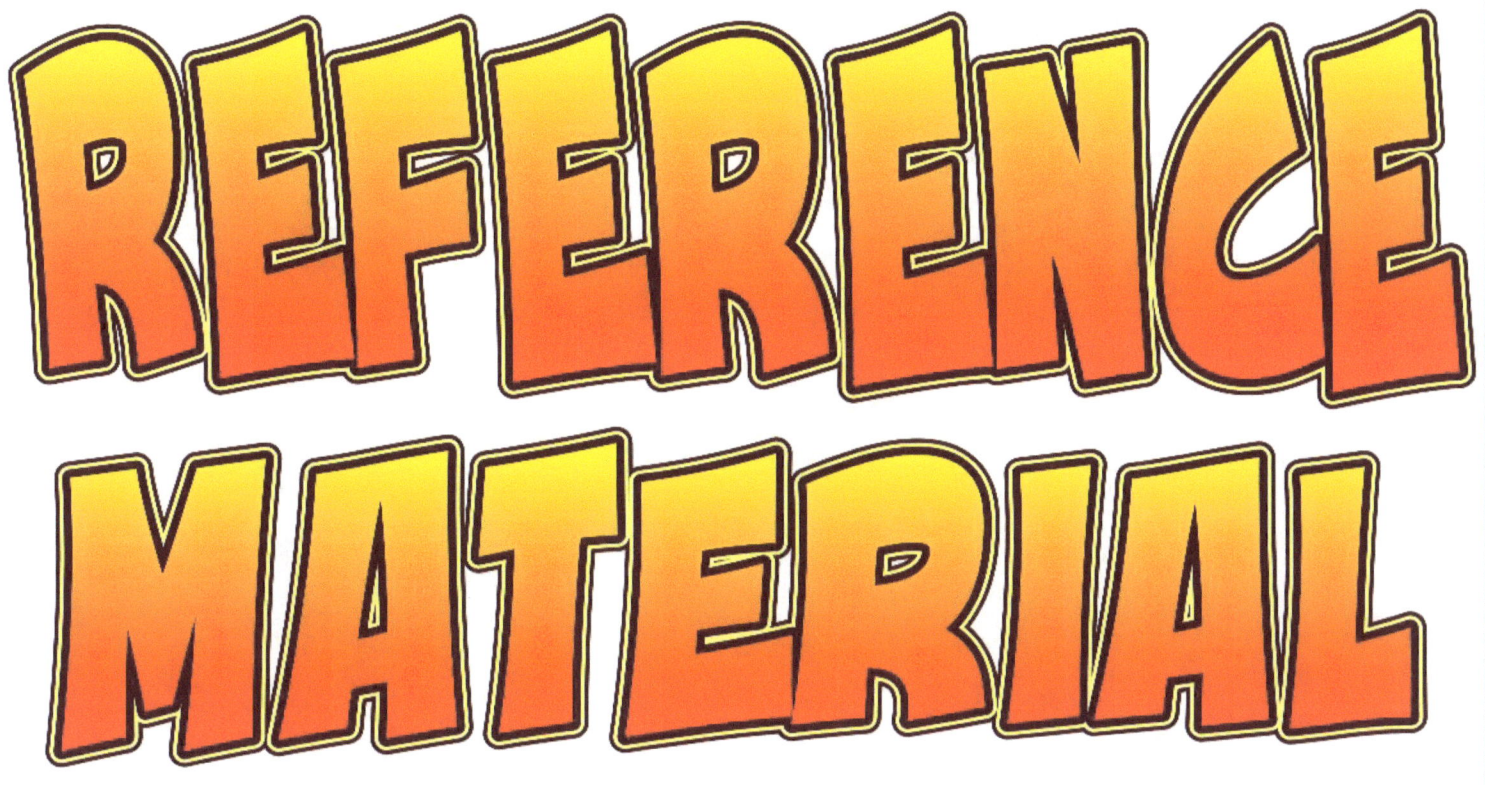

REFERENCE MATERIAL

ALL THIS MEANS IS...TAKE NOTES... SKETCH, TAKE PHOTOS, STUDY YOUR FAVORITE ARTISTS STYLES.

SEE WHAY YOU LIKE AND DO WHAT YOU LIKE TO DO.

BE THE 'GO TO' GUY.

ALWAYS MEET YOUR DEADLINES!

BE PROFESSIONAL.

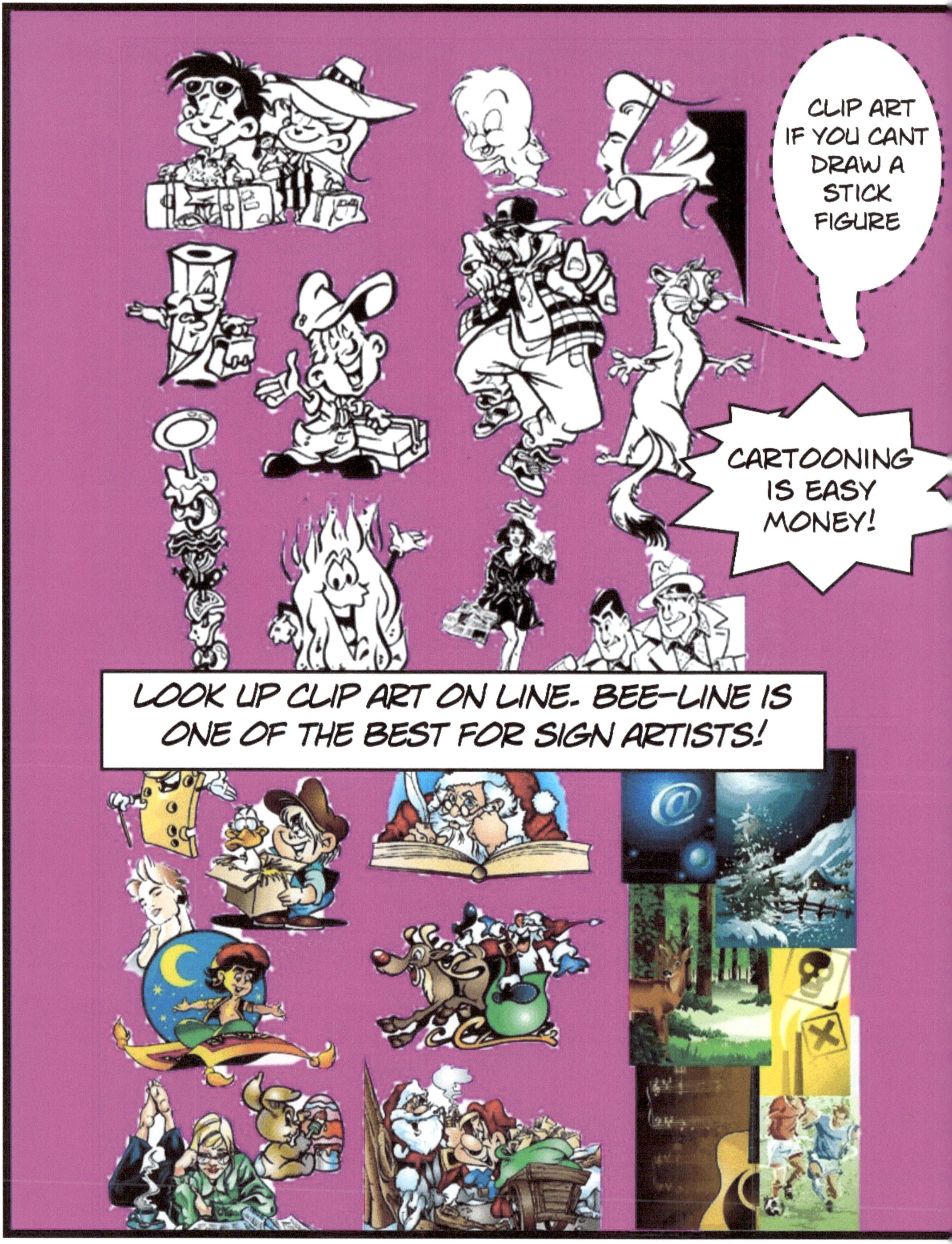

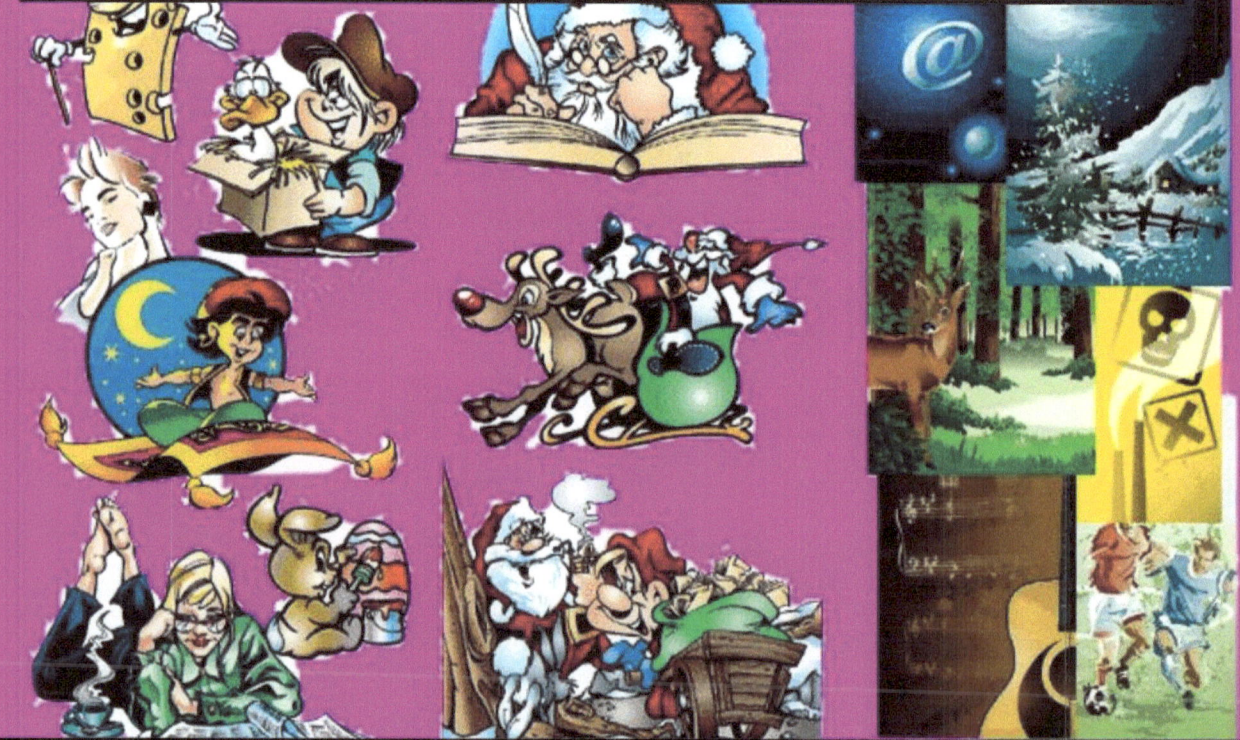

CLIP ART IF YOU CANT DRAW A STICK FIGURE

CARTOONING IS EASY MONEY!

LOOK UP CLIP ART ON LINE. BEE-LINE IS ONE OF THE BEST FOR SIGN ARTISTS!

DO I REALLY NEED TO KNOW ANATOMY?

NO YOU DON'T!
USE SIMPLE SHAPES
CIRCLES, SQUARES, TRIANGLES
TO MAKE UP THE SHAPES OF THE FACE
AND BODY.
IT'S EASY TO CARTOON IF YOU JUST
DRAW A STICK MAN THE HEAD IS
REALLY ALL YOU GOT TO WORRY
ABOUT!

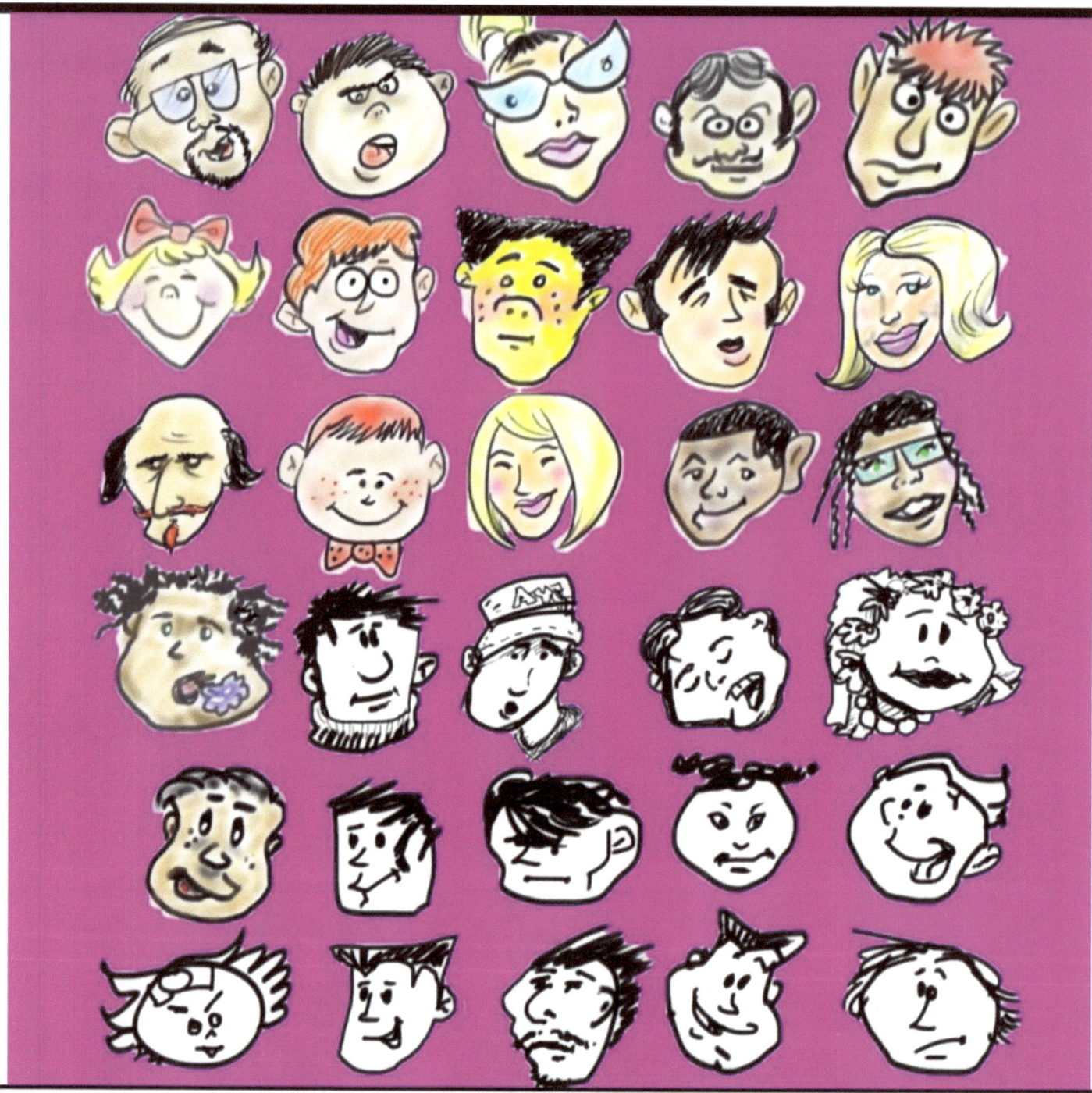

DRAWING IS EASY, JUST DRAW A CIRCLE AND GO FROM THERE, ADD COLOR AND SHADING, AND WAALA!
E-BOOKS SELL THEMSELVES!

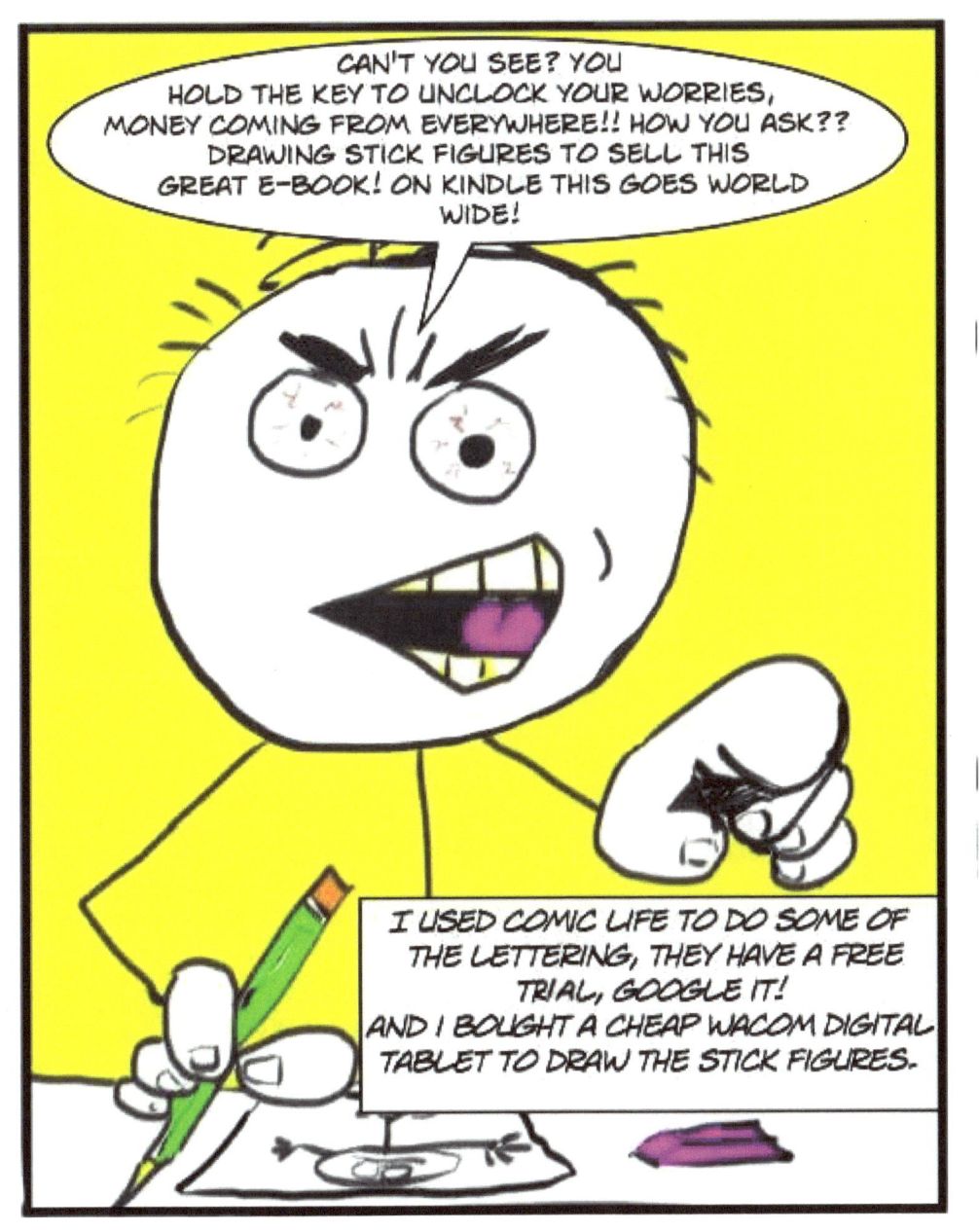

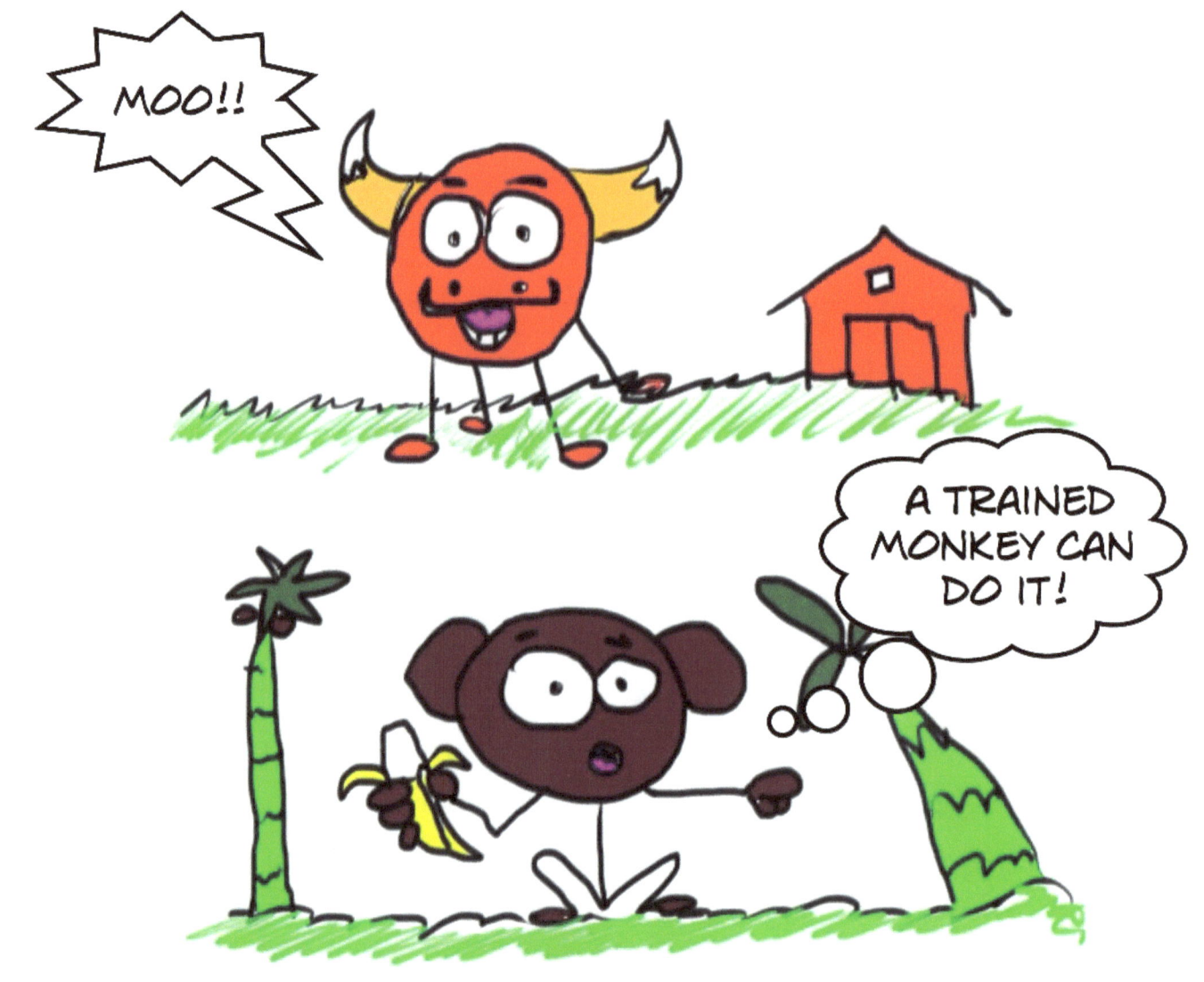

ANIMALS PEOPLE, STICK
FIGURES...
HOW EASY IS THAT??

THIS COULD START A WAVE OF
AWESOME E-BOOKS!

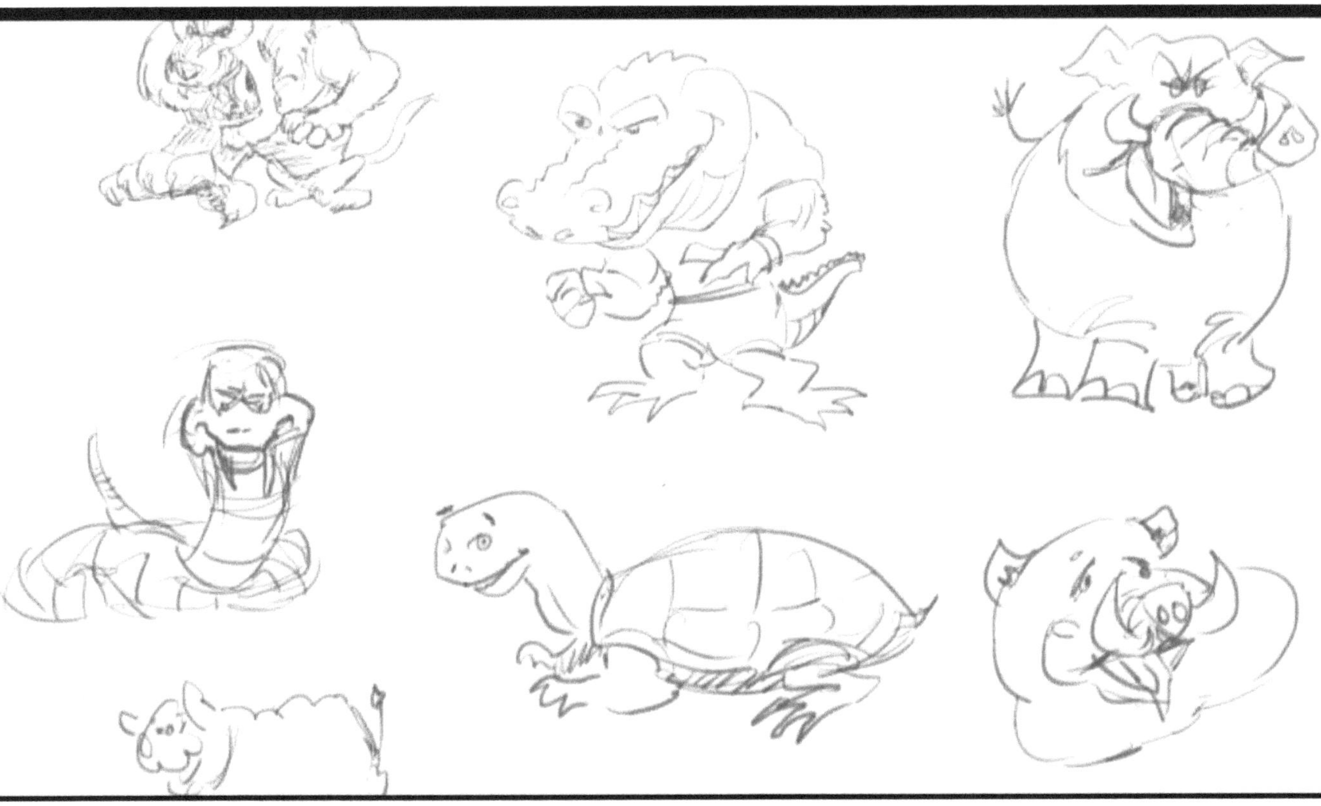

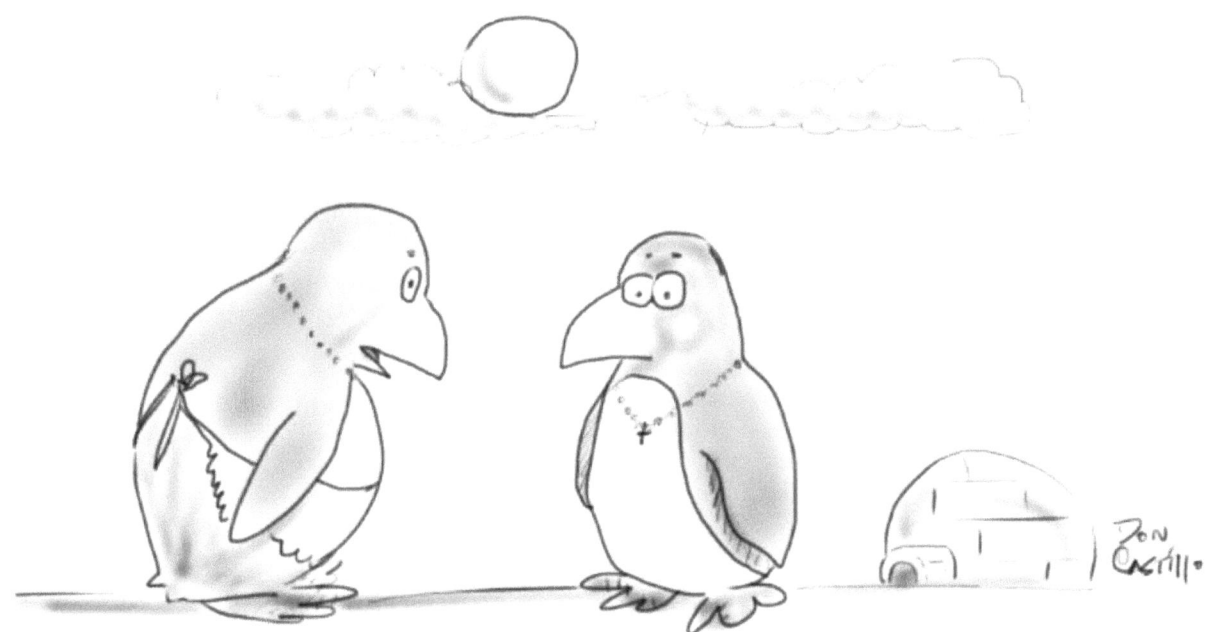

ILLUSTRATE A CHILDREN'S BOOK, SEND CARTOONS YOU DO TO CERTAIN MARKETS OR MAGAZINES, MANY CAN BE SUBMITTED ON LINE SAVING YOU POSTAGE!

AND When you get to Heaven, You get wings that actually work!

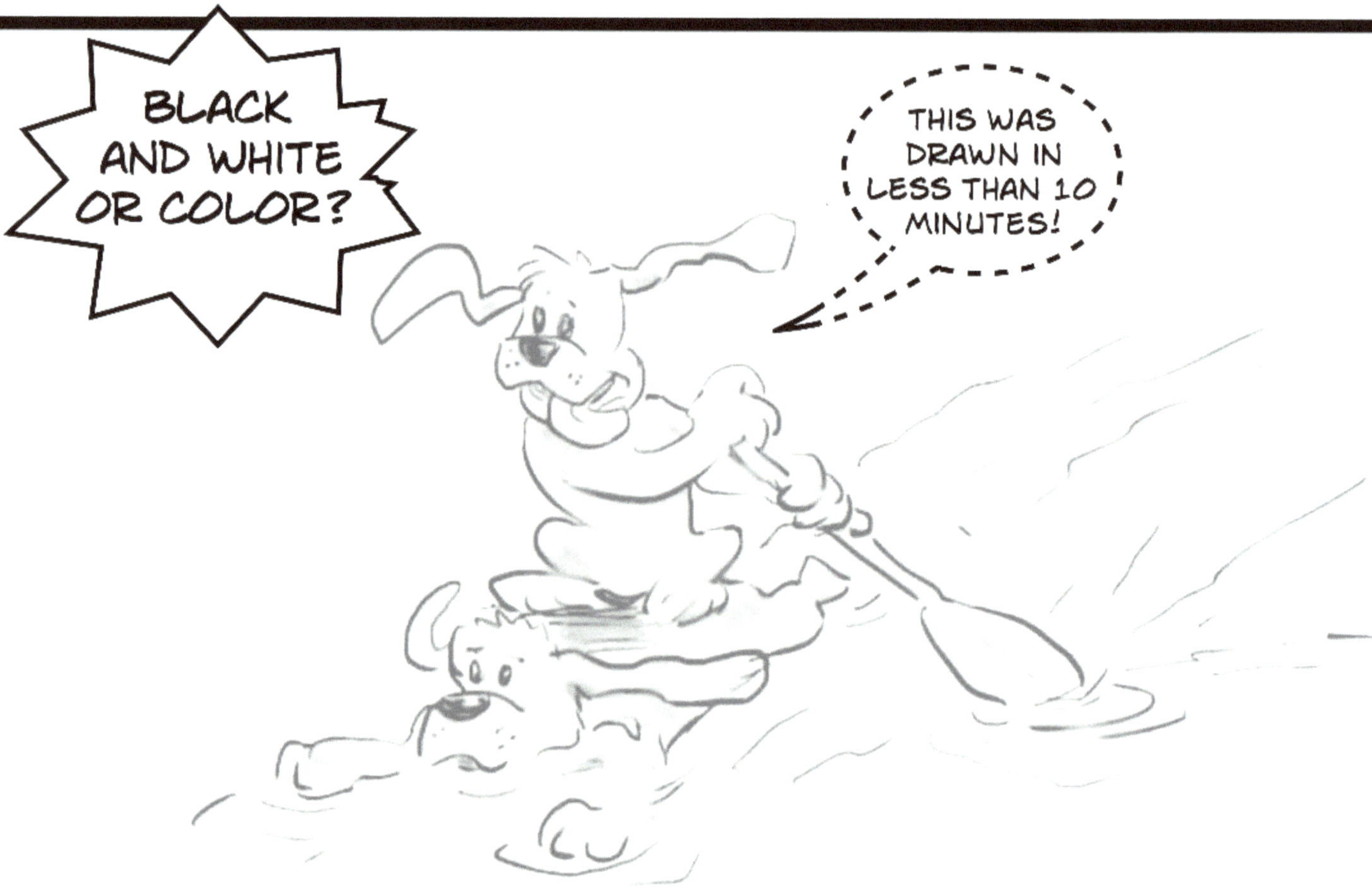

YOU CAN SEE HOW ANY E-BOOK WOULD MAKE TONS OF MONEY IF THEY USED SIMPLE CARTOONS TO ILLUSTRATE A STORY.

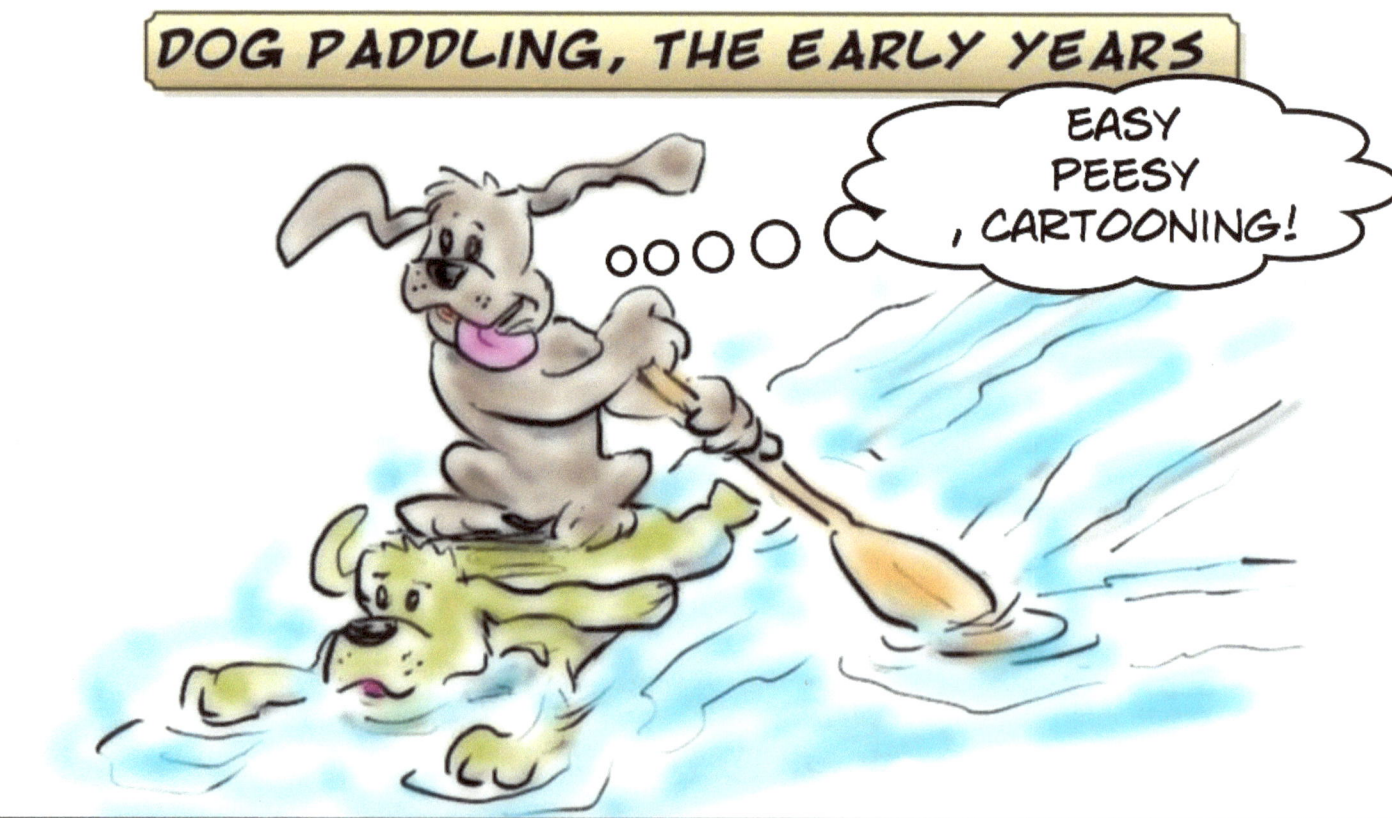

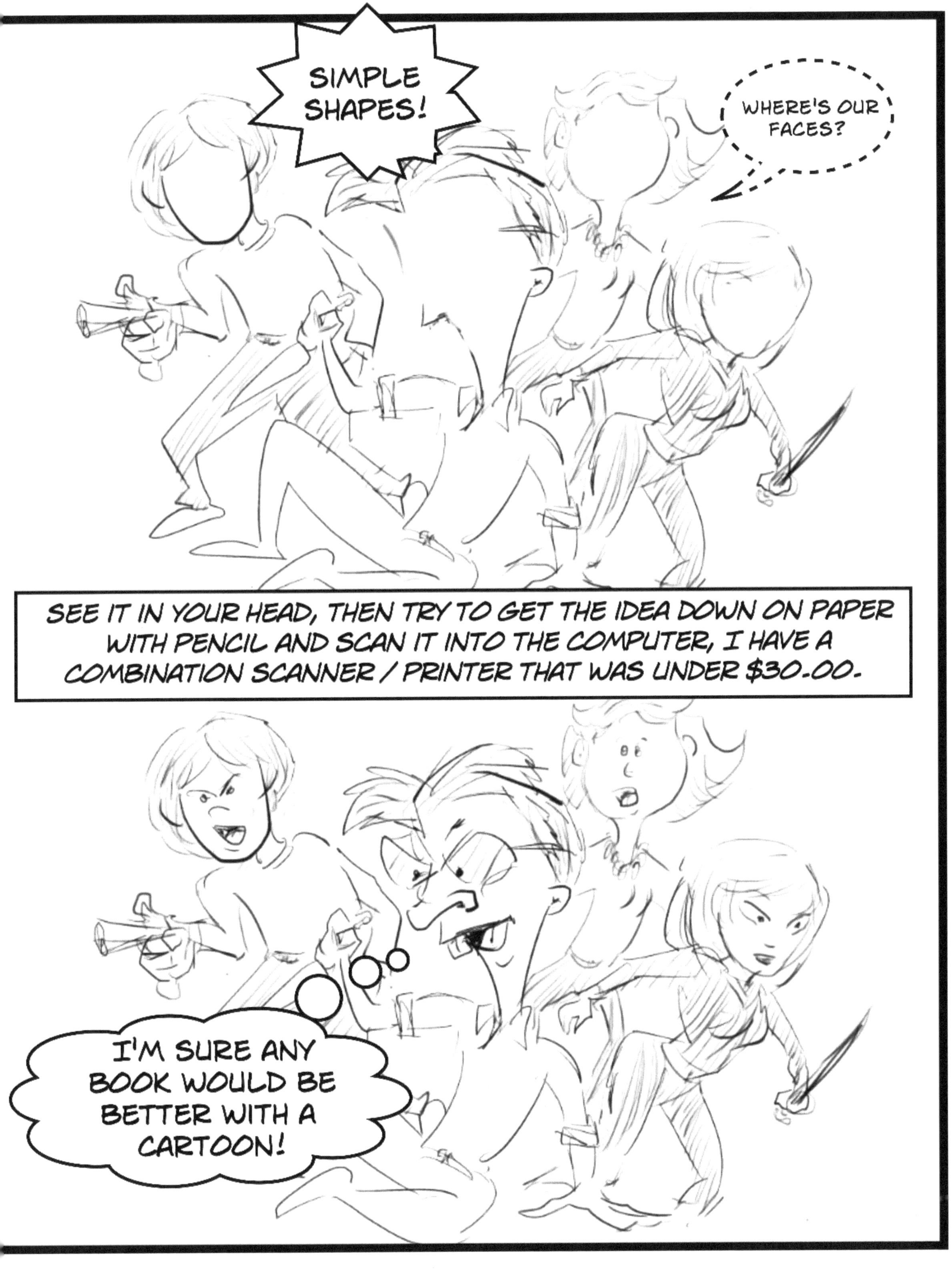

SIMPLE SHAPES!

WHERE'S OUR FACES?

SEE IT IN YOUR HEAD, THEN TRY TO GET THE IDEA DOWN ON PAPER WITH PENCIL AND SCAN IT INTO THE COMPUTER, I HAVE A COMBINATION SCANNER / PRINTER THAT WAS UNDER $30.00.

I'M SURE ANY BOOK WOULD BE BETTER WITH A CARTOON!

SKETCHBOOK PRO

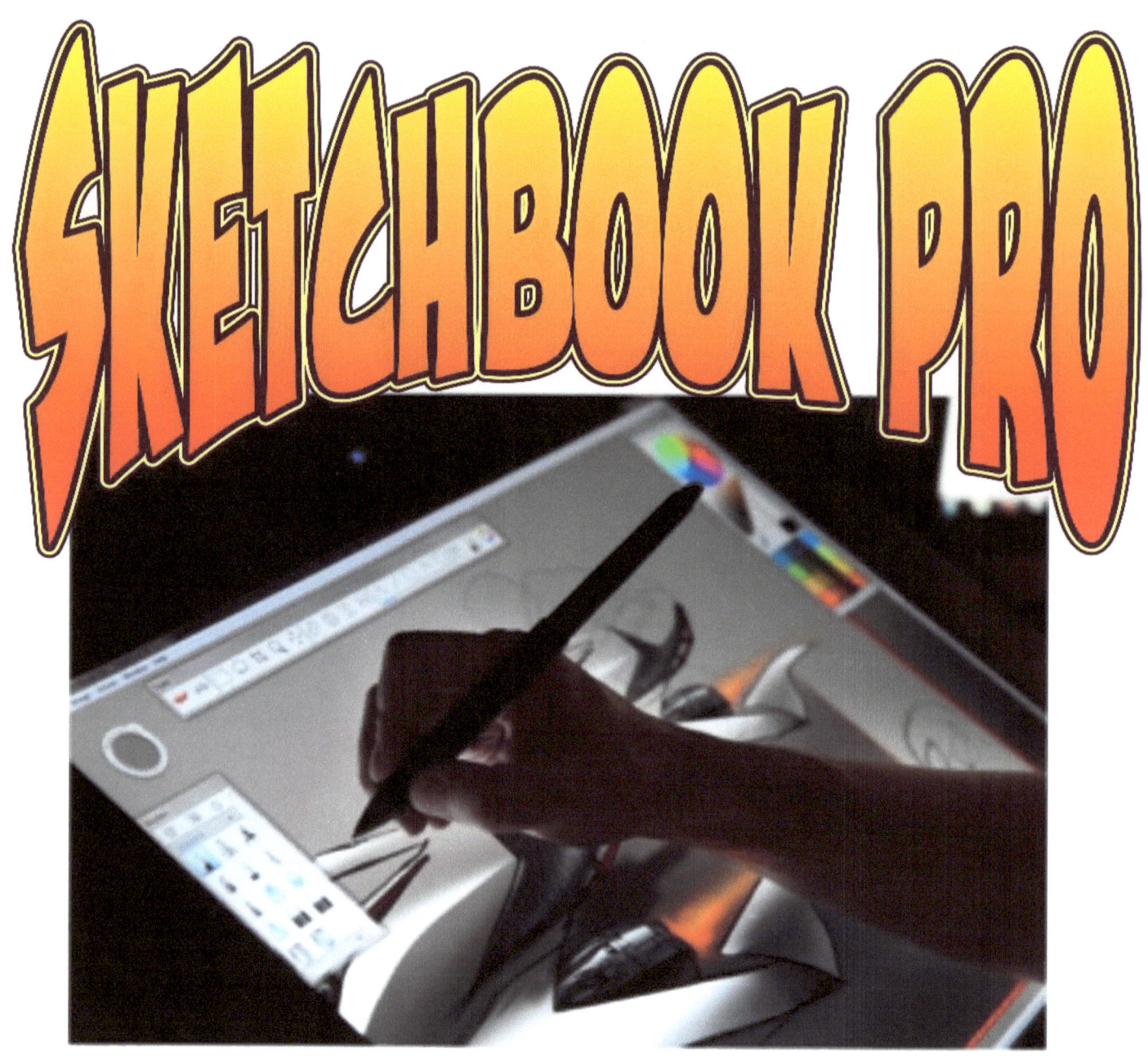

SKETCHBOOK PRO IS WHAT I USE TO DRAW DIGITALLY, NO PAPER, NO MESS! THEY ALSO HAVE A FREE TRIAL SO GOOGLE IT!

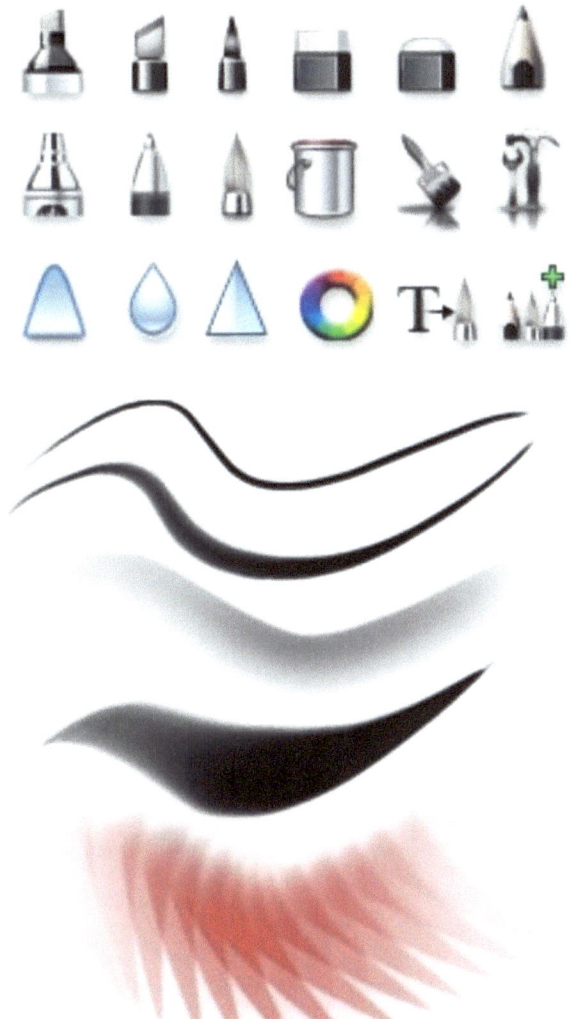

SKETCHBOOK PRO

THESE ARE SOME OF THE EFFECTS
YOU CAN USE ON SKETCHBOOK PRO.
MESS FREE MATERIALS

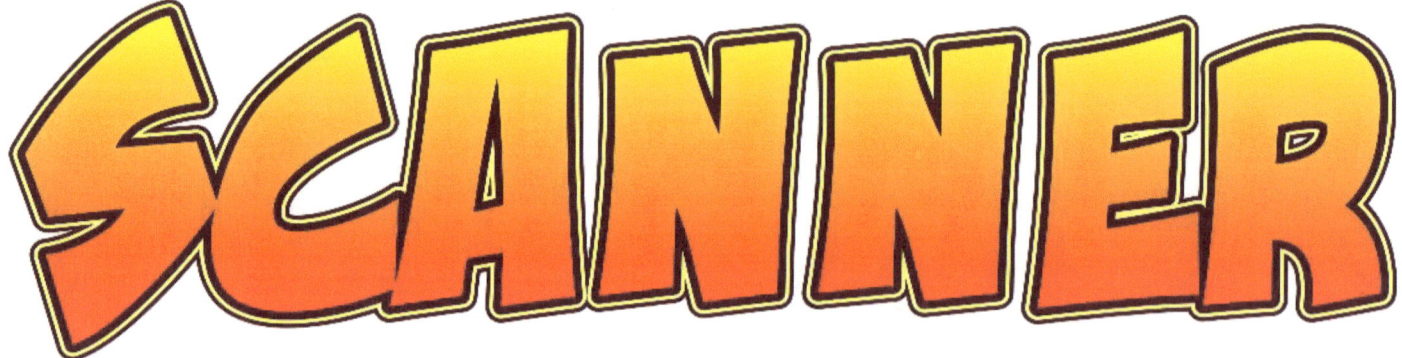

SCANNER

A SCANNER IS HANDY TO HAVE TO SCAN PHOTOS AND PRINT COPIES OF CONTRACTS ETC.

YOU CAN ALSO PRINT WITH SOME MODELS AND THATS GREAT FOR PRINTING PROMOTIONAL MATERIALS TO HELP YOU MAKE MORE MONEY!

WACOM BAMBOO DIGITAL TABLET

USE THIS TO MAKE MESS FREE DRAWINGS! TAKES A LITTLE WHILE TO GET USED TO, BUT WELL WORTH IT!

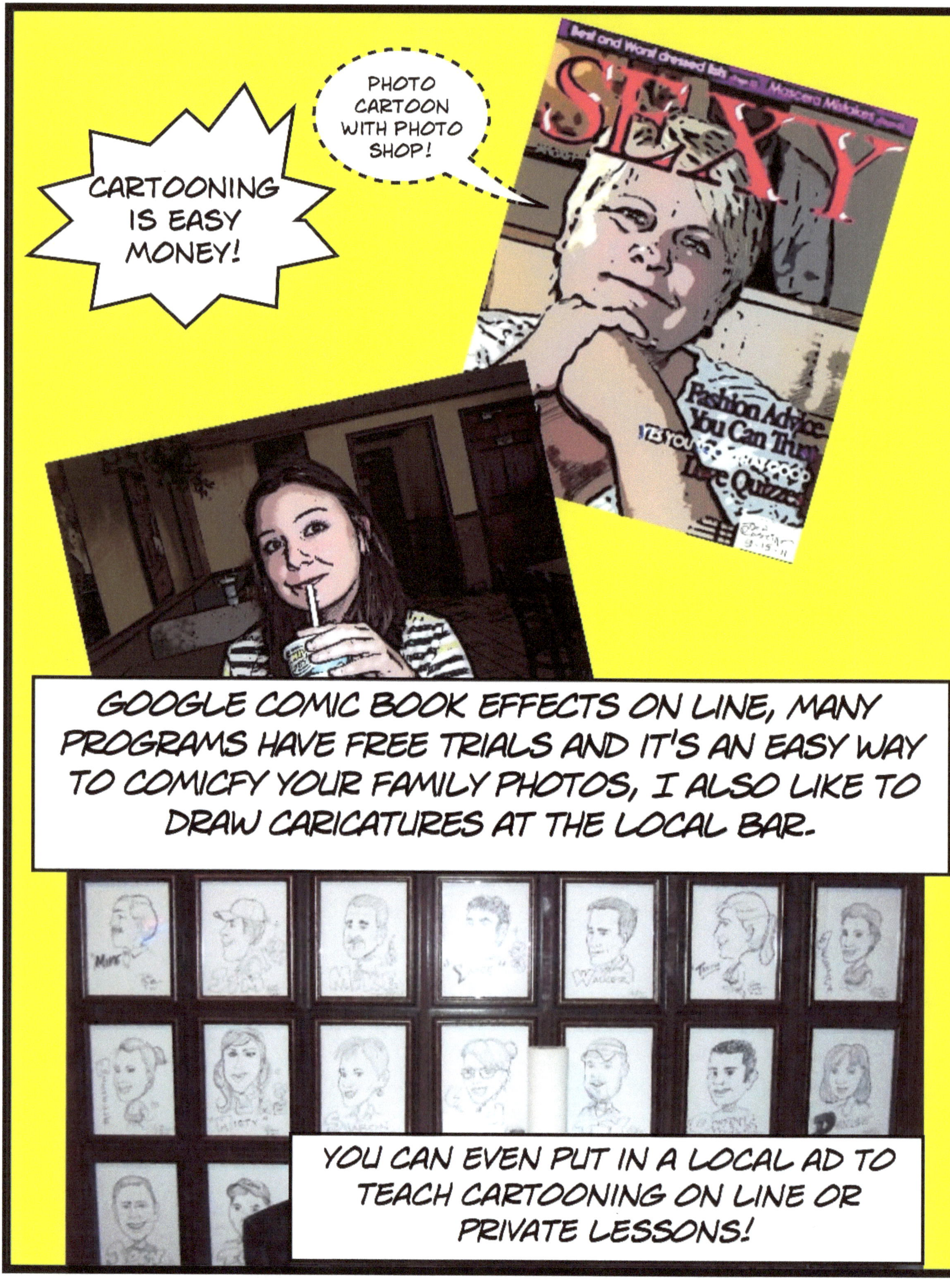

CARTOONING IS EASY MONEY!

PHOTO CARTOON WITH PHOTO SHOP!

SEXY

Best and Worst dressed lists

Mascara Misfortunes

Fashion Advice You Can Trust

Love Quizzes

GOOGLE COMIC BOOK EFFECTS ON LINE, MANY PROGRAMS HAVE FREE TRIALS AND IT'S AN EASY WAY TO COMICFY YOUR FAMILY PHOTOS, I ALSO LIKE TO DRAW CARICATURES AT THE LOCAL BAR.

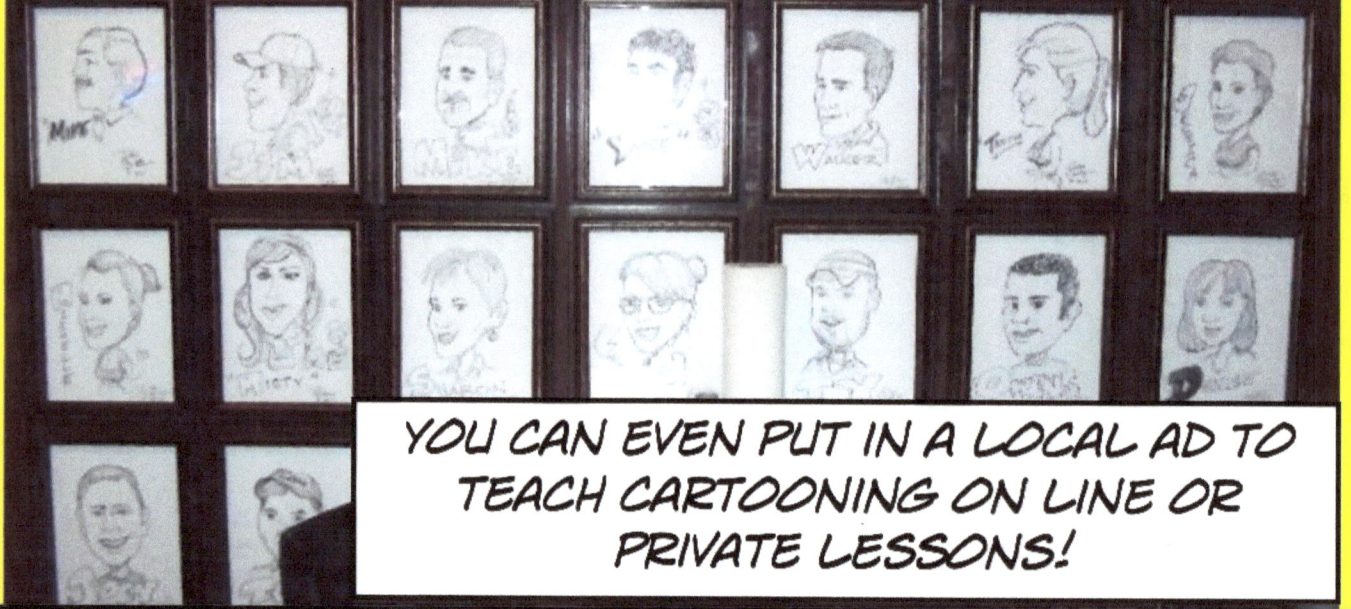

YOU CAN EVEN PUT IN A LOCAL AD TO TEACH CARTOONING ON LINE OR PRIVATE LESSONS!

FIND YOUR PERSONAL STYLE

AFTER A WHILE YOU DRAWINGS WILL TAKE ON A 'STYLE' ALL THEIR OWN, MAKE SURE YOU DON'T ALWAYS COPY LINE FOR LINE. MAKE IT YOUR OWN!

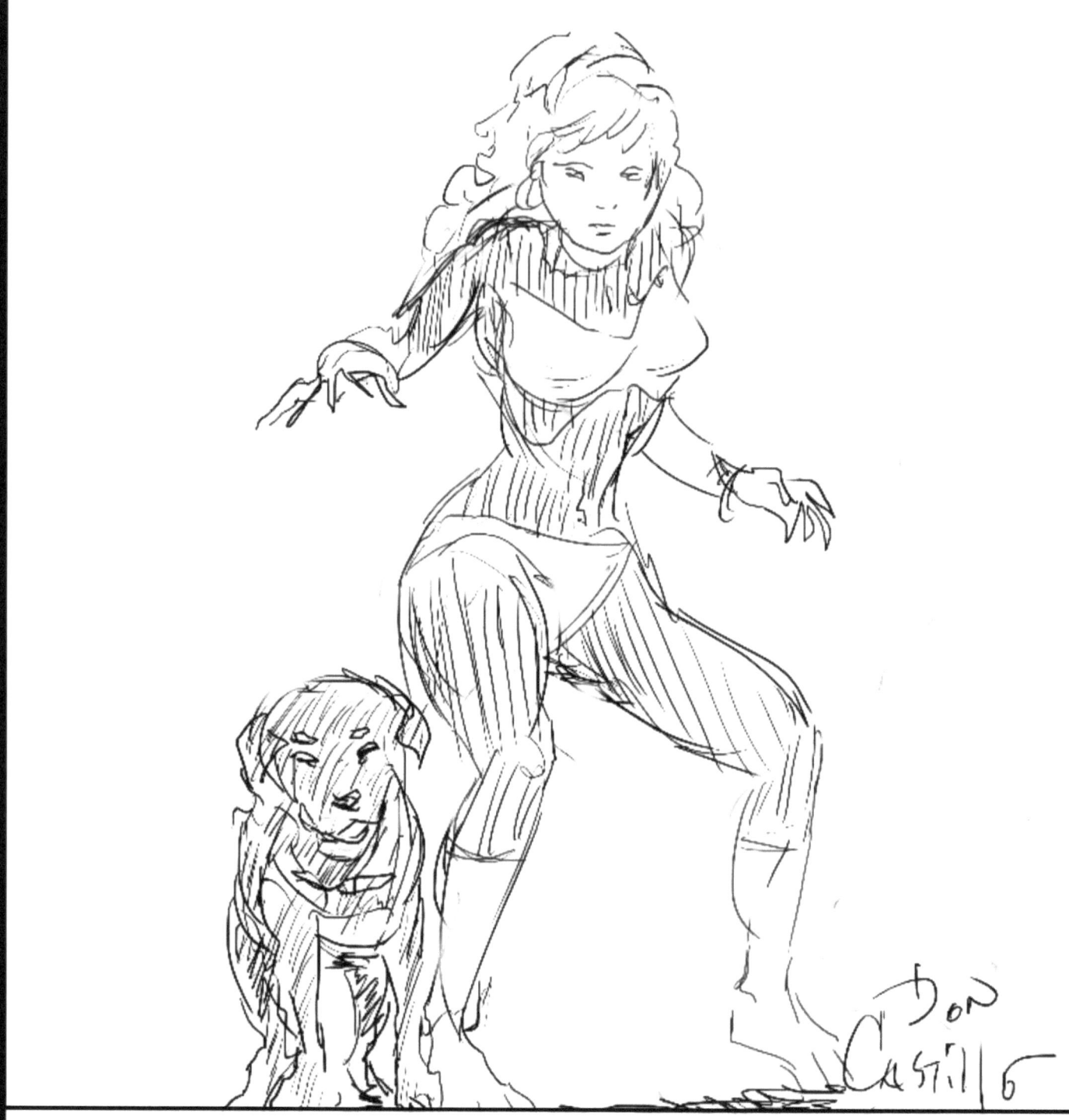

SIMPLE LINE DRAWING CAN BE USED TO MAKE COMIC BOOKS AND SOLD TO YOUR FRIENDS! EASY MONEY!

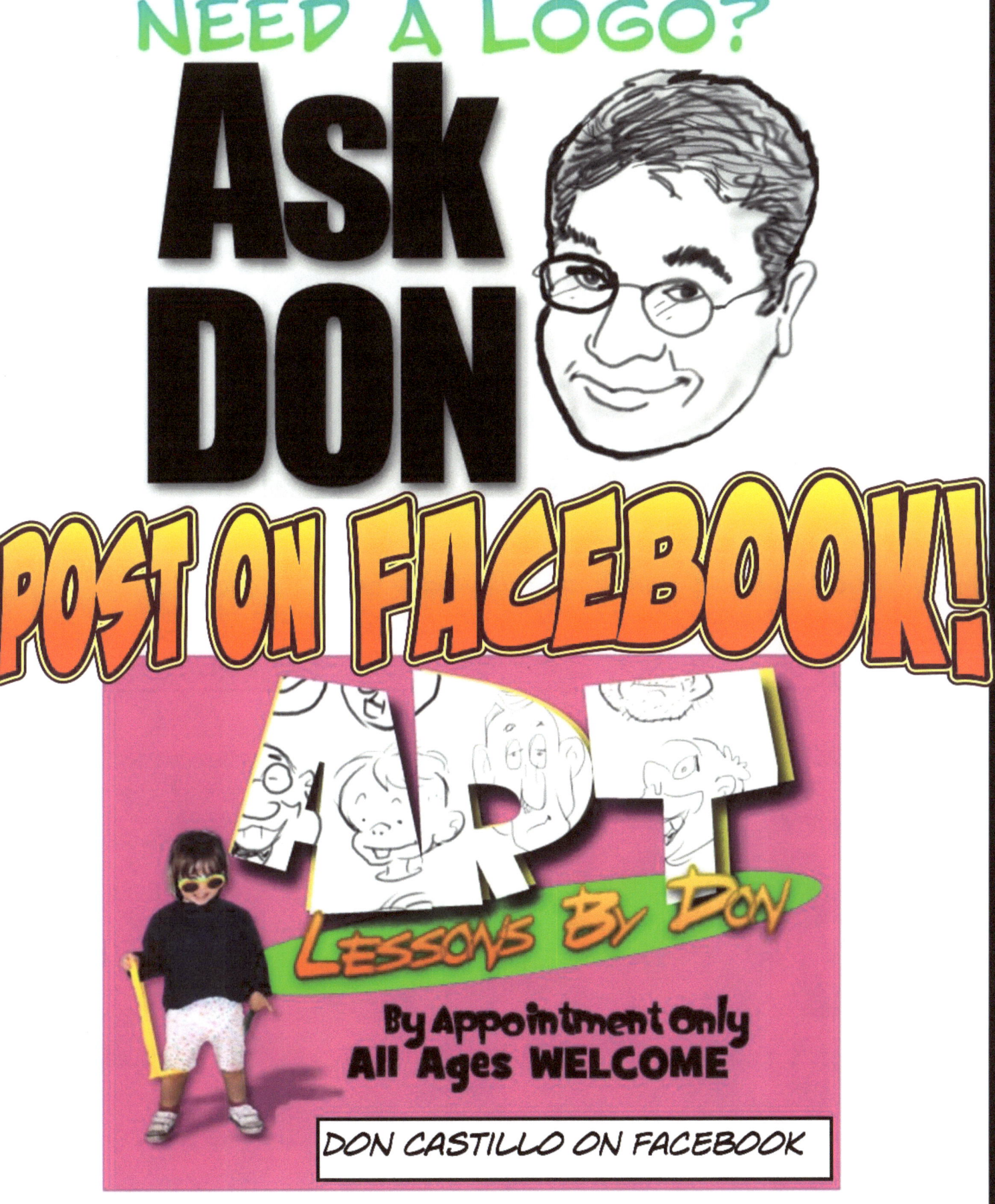

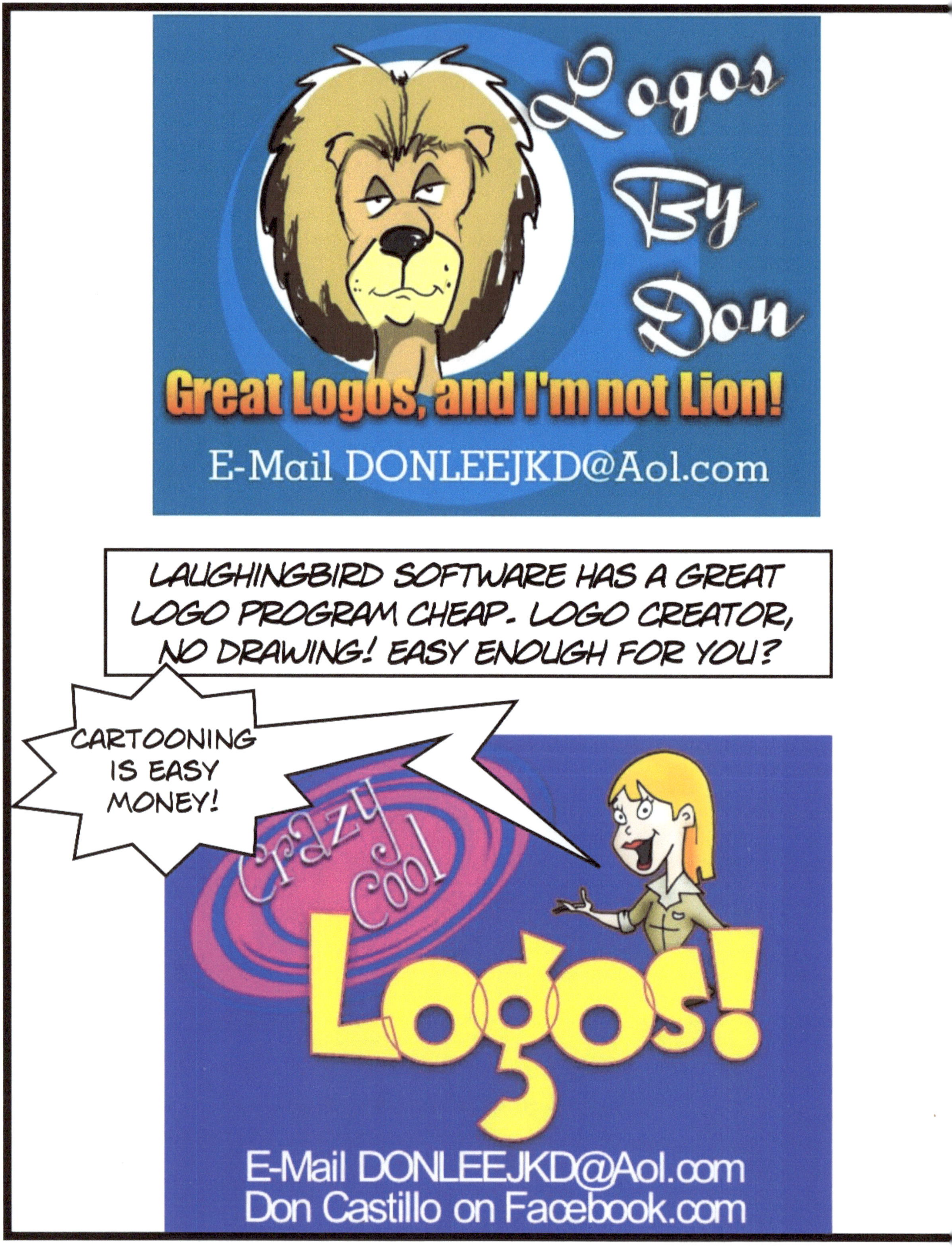

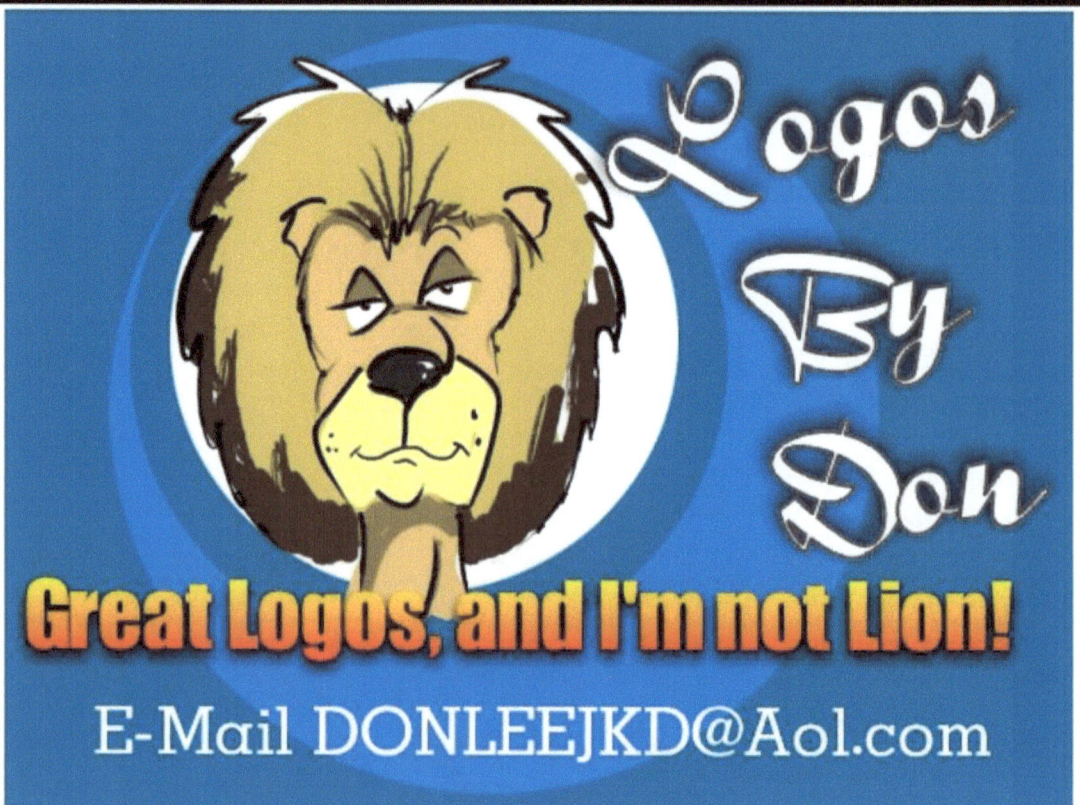

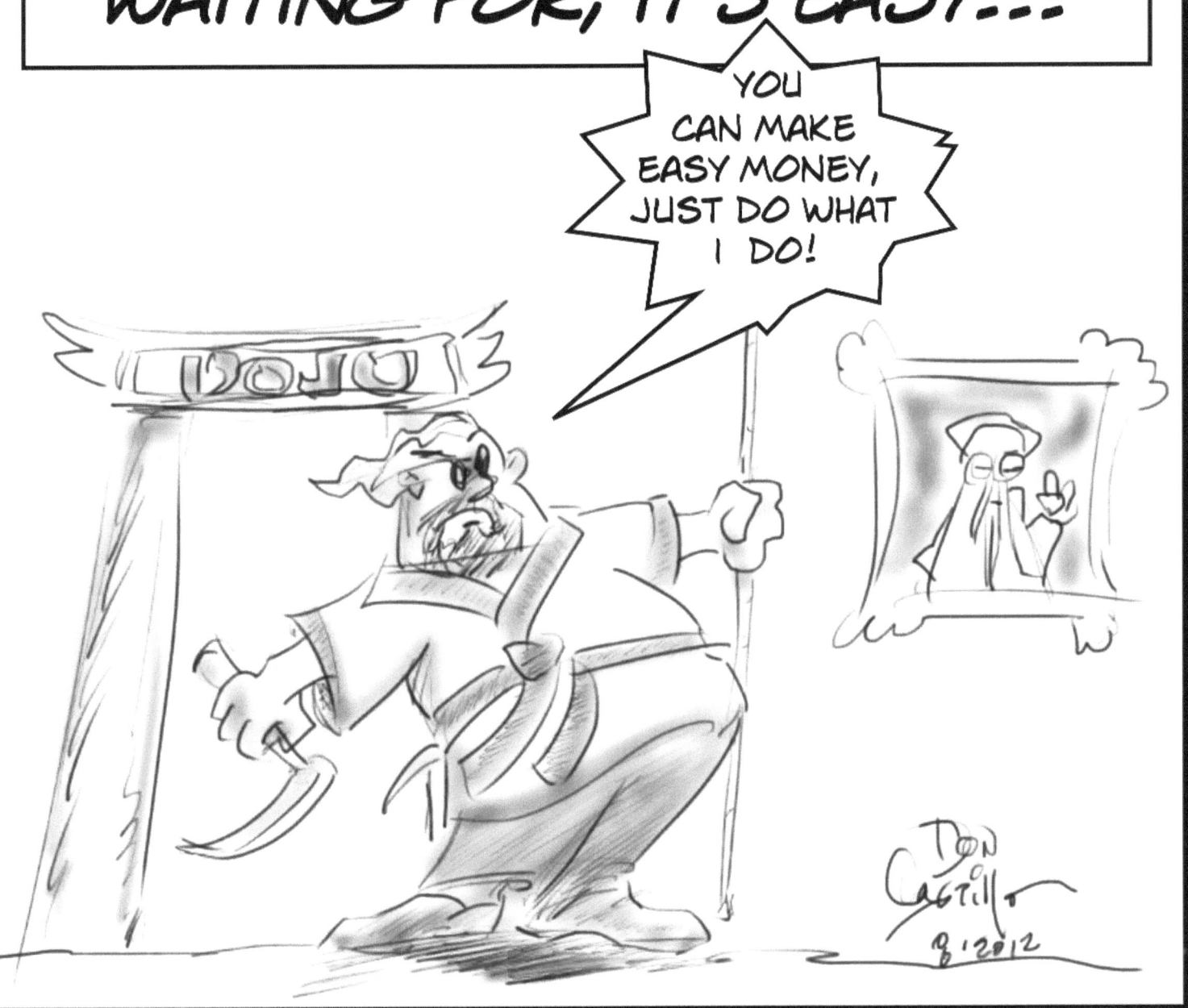

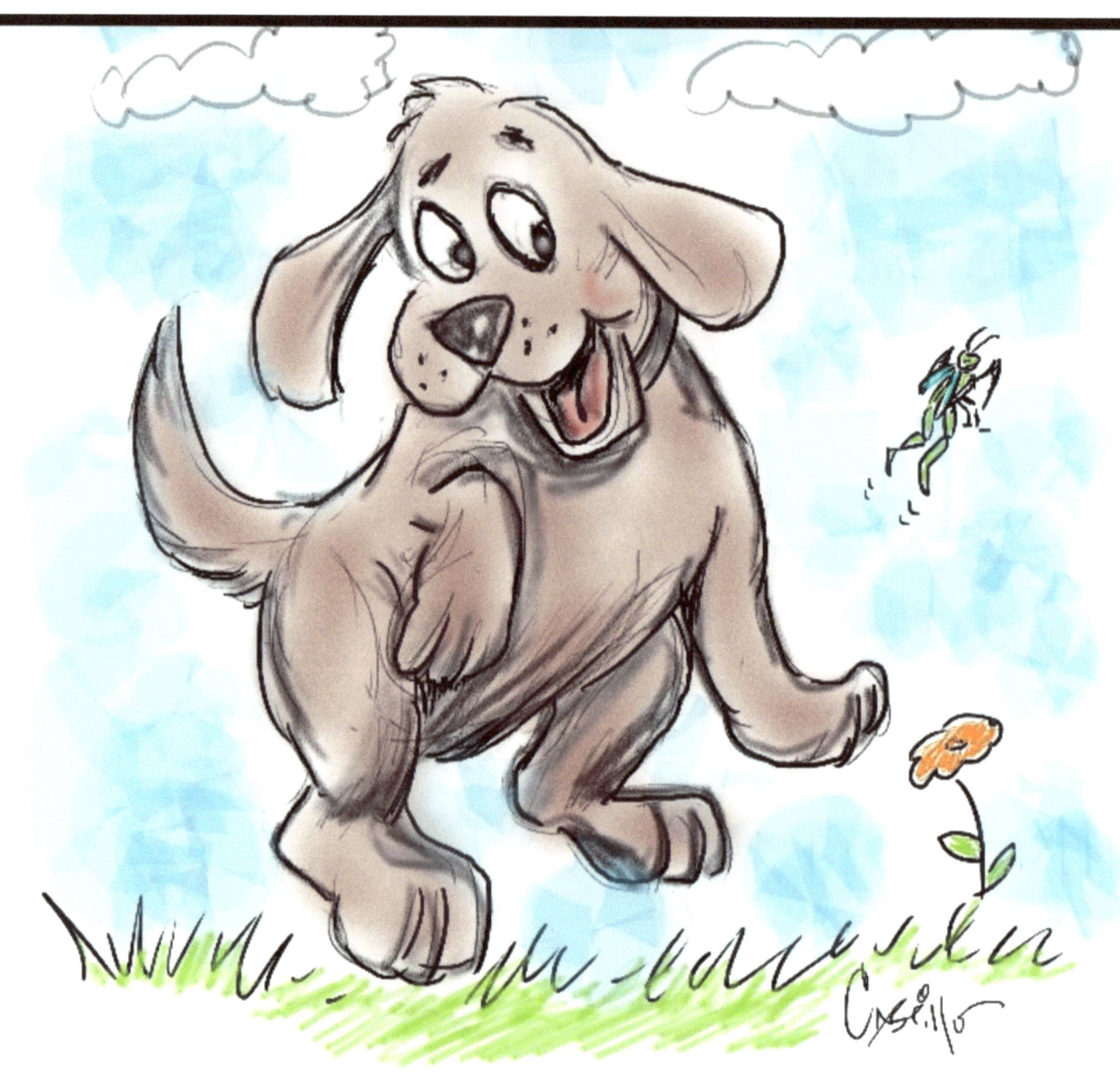

PET SHOPS, PEST CONTROL, LAWN CARE, ANY OF THOSE BUSINESSES WOULD LOVE TO USE A CARTOON FOR THEIR ADVERTISING!

CONCLUSION

I HOPE YOU ENJOYED MY BOOK, AND I REALLY HOPE YOU USE THE INFORMATION TO MAKE TONS OF CASH!

REMEMBER ME WHEN YOU MAKE IT BIG!

I WISH TO DEDICATE THIS TO MY LOVING WIFE TAMMY AND OUR WONDERFUL FAMILY.
MAKING MONEY IS EASY! JUST DO WHAT I DID!

DRAW YOURSELF AS A CARTOON, USE IT TO MARKET YOURSELF!

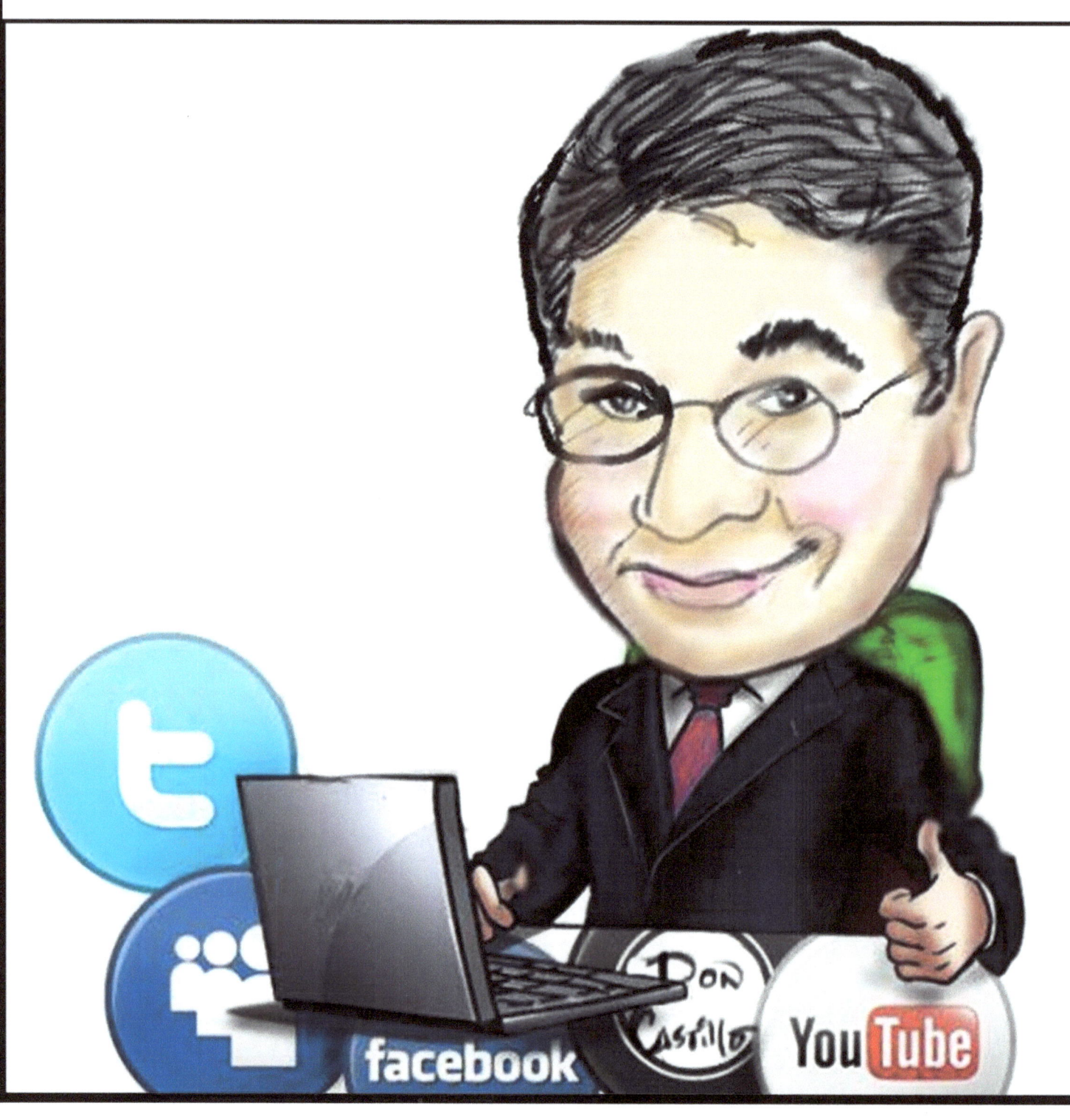

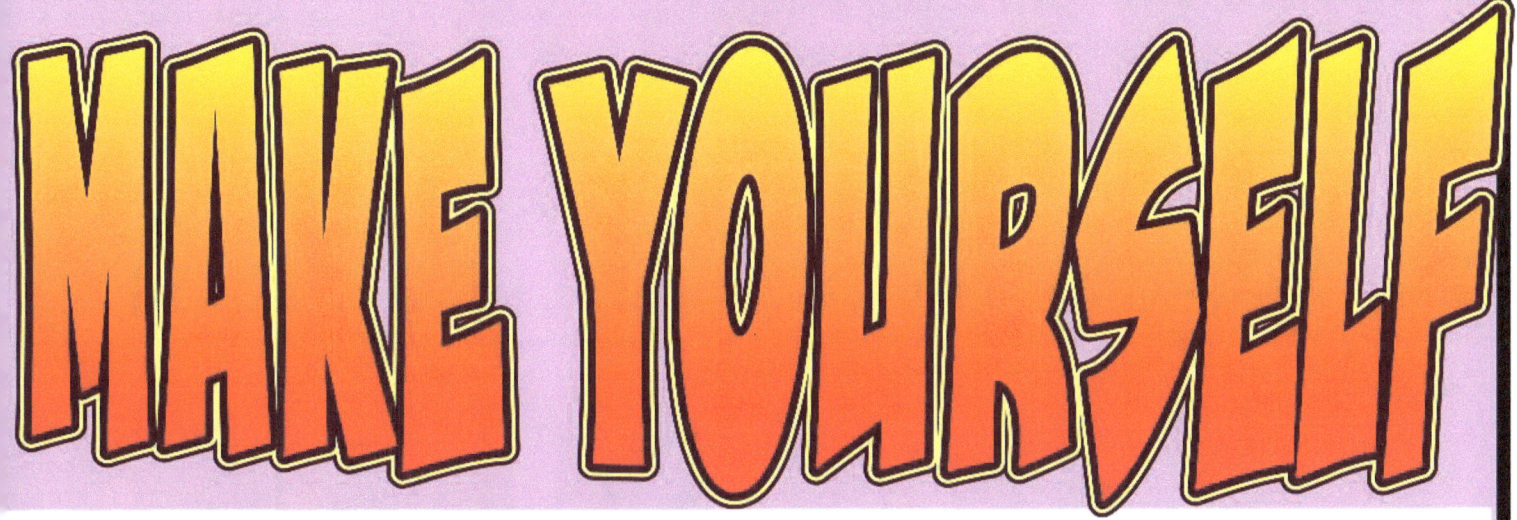

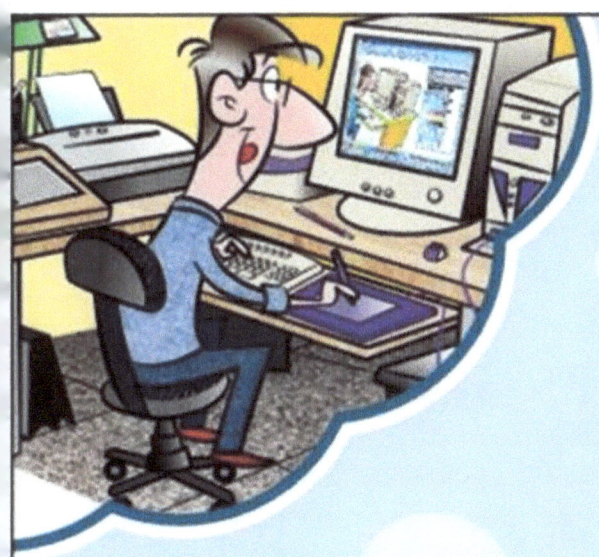

Art By Don
Caricatures or Art Lessons Also Available For Parties and
Company Events
Don Lee Castillo
Owner / Artist

2211 4th Ave. North
Clanton, Al
35045
205 258-5036
Private Lessons Available
DonLeeJKD@aol.com
on FaceBook at Art Lessons in Clanton, Alabama

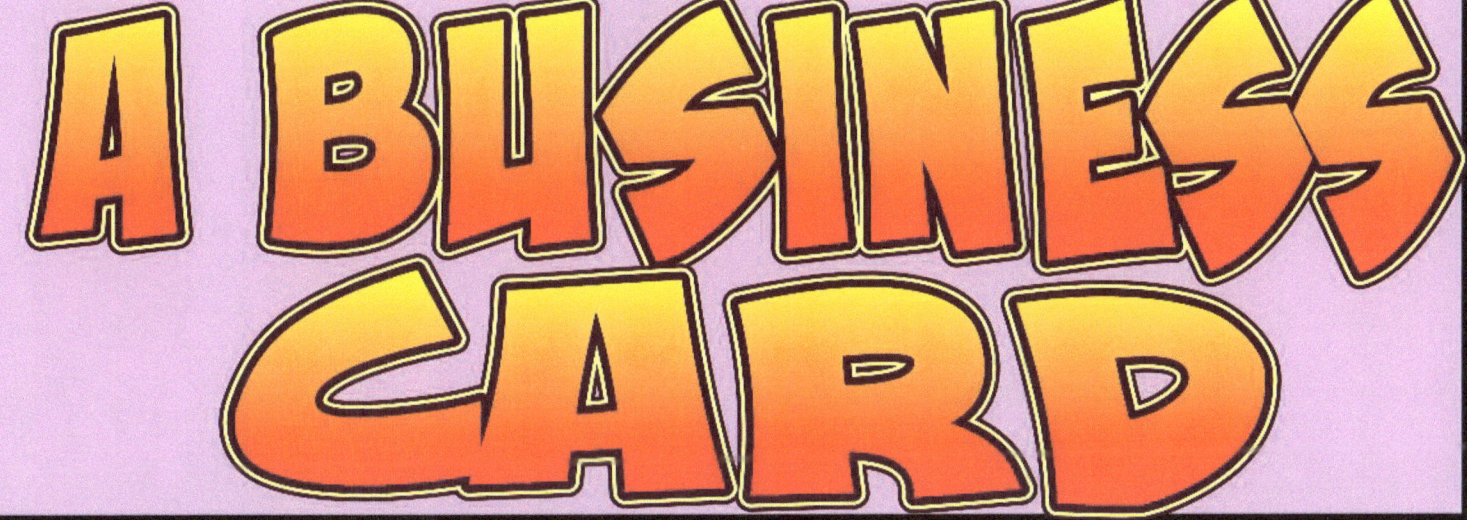

MAKING MONEY WITH E-BOOKS AND AD'S IS EASY, ALL YOU GOTTA DO IS WHAT I DO, MAKE A BOOK, SELL IT ON LINE AND MAKE TONS OF CASH!

E-MAIL ME AT DONLEEJKD@AOL.COM OR DON CASTILLO ON FACEBOOK
AND ALWAYS BE POSITIVE IN WHAT YOU DO, SUCESS WILL COME.

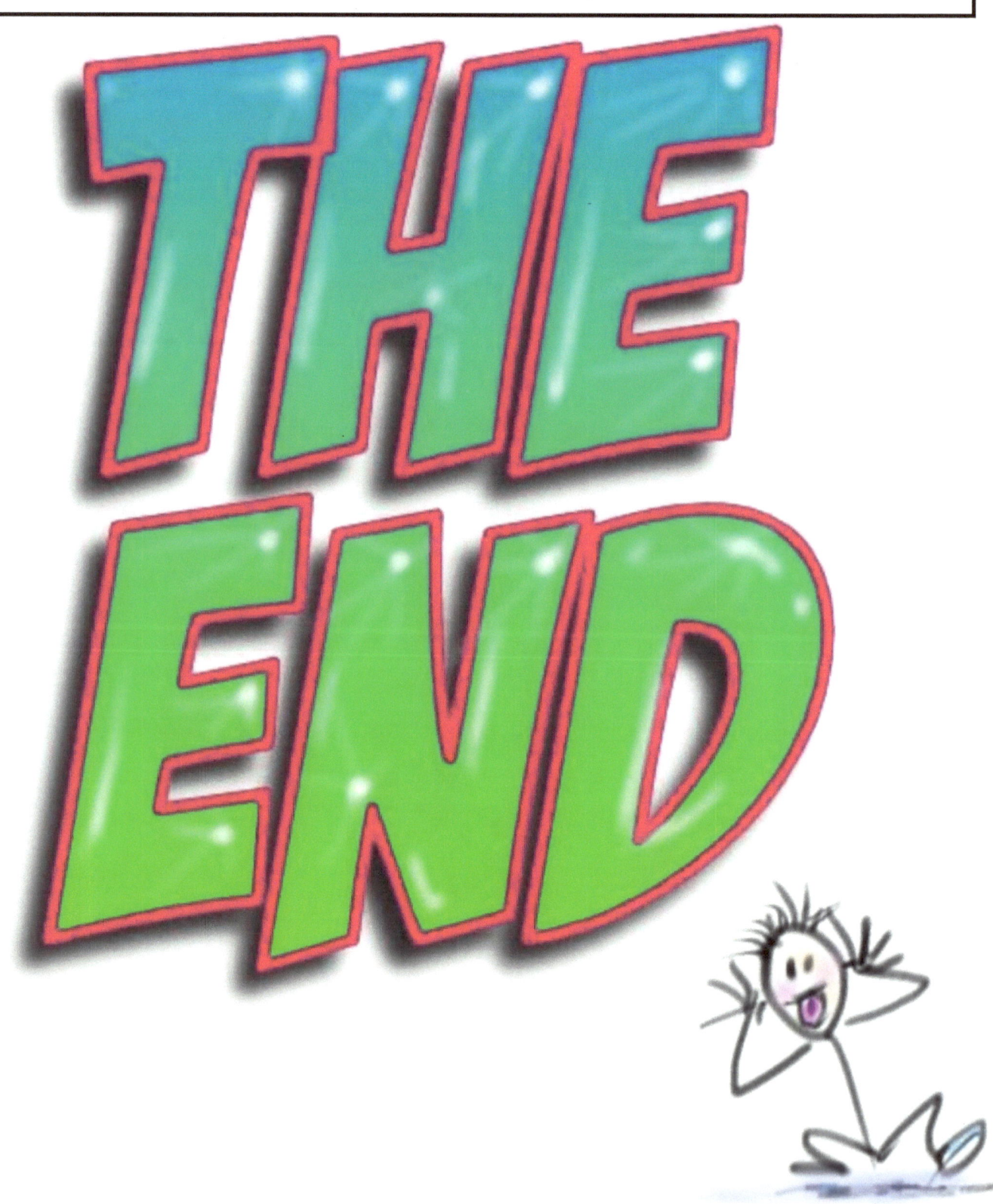

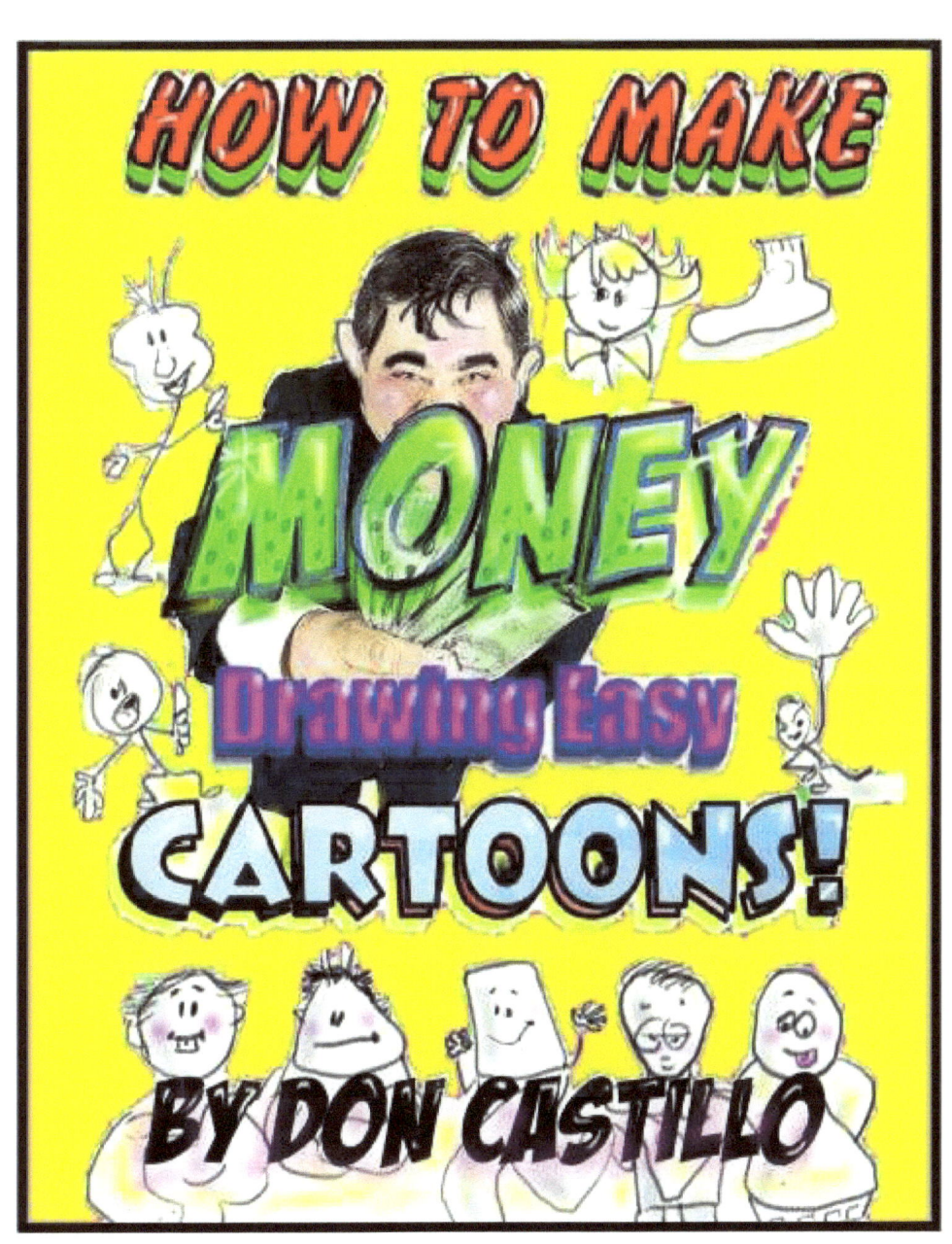